GROWING HERBS

Roy Genders

Series Editor
Professor Alan Gemmell

Illustrations by
Vanessa Pancheri

TEACH YOURSELF BOOKS
Hodder and Stoughton

First printed 1980

Published in the USA by David McKay & Co. Inc.,
750 Third Avenue, New York, NY 10017, USA.

British Library C.I.P.

Genders, Roy
    Growing herbs. – (Teach yourself books).
    1. Herb gardening
    I. Title   II. Series
    635′.7   SB351.H5

    ISBN 0–340–247878

Printed and bound in Great Britain for Hodder and Stoughton paperbacks, a division of Hodder and Stoughton Ltd, Mill Road, Dunton Green, Sevenoaks, Kent, (Editorial Office: 47 Bedford Square, London, WC1B 3DP) by Richard Clay (The Chaucer Press) Ltd, Bungay, Suffolk

GROWING HERBS

Roy Genders is a Yorkshireman who has spent his whole life growing fruits, leeks and vegetables and devoting his time to most other aspects of gardening.

For many years he was a commercial grower of fruit and vegetables, cultivating a large acreage in Somerset. He still spends a lot of time in his garden, trying out new varieties and comparing them with the old ones, the results of which he makes mention in the articles he writes for leading magazines and in the numerous books he has written.

Among his books are included *The Scented Wild Flowers of Britain* (Collins), *The History of Scent* (Hamish Hamilton), *Wild Life in the Garden* (Faber and Faber), *The Scented Flora of the World* (Robert Hale and St Martin's Press) and *Growing Fruit* in this Teach Yourself Series. He is also known for his radio broadcasts and television shows.

TEACH YOURSELF BOOKS

Contents

Introduction

When man first came to inhabit the earth, he learnt to rely upon certain plants for his health and to supply his food. The conifers provided him with a balsamic gum which exuded from the bark and which was used to cleanse the body and to heal wounds made by his simple tools or in combat. Later, as other plants came to be appreciated both for culinary and medicinal uses, they took on a special meaning, they were acclaimed for the contribution they made to the life-style of simple men. Angelica for instance, a plant of extreme hardiness, which grows wild in Iceland and Scandinavia, was so highly regarded by the Vikings and Norsemen, that it was thought to be a plant of heavenly origin. To this day, the Dutch call it 'the plant of the Holy Ghost'. It is a carminative, it helps the digestion, and, in mediaeval times, the roots were chewed as they were thought to ward off the plague. The seeds were burned in pans on a low fire when they would scent musty smelling houses, with their damp earth floors, with a delicious fragrance, and the stems, stewed with crab apples, rhubarb and other fruits of the countryside, would give them a pleasant musky flavour. From the roots, boiled in water, a drink is obtained which, sweetened with honey, is sleep-inducing; it aids a hard cough and relieves a bronchial chest. Taken regularly, it will relieve gout and rheumatic pains so that it is no wonder the plant was thought of as a gift from heaven. There were other plants such as bistort, the juice of which healed body sores, and rubbed on to the gums, brought relief to aching teeth, while the dried root, powdered and taken in wine or water 'doth wonderfully stop the spitting of blood'. It was also a reliable cure for jaundice.

Many other countryside plants, which were later grown in cottage gardens, possessed similar valuable qualities. Anglo-Saxon leech books, used by those who administered to the sick, tell of the value of brooklime, an insignificant little plant which grows in ditches, for maintaining a healthy body and, during Elizabethan times, Gerard in his *Herbal* (1596) tells that it prevented scurvy which modern scientists have shown is due to the lack of vitamin C in the diet. Only recently has it become known that brooklime has a high vitamin C content.

Farm workers would place the leaves of borage in their sandwiches for they knew that it would revive them after a long morning's work, without knowing that the plant is rich in potassium salts which have the power of invigoration. The Greeks of ancient Athens ate it when training for the Olympic Games and named the plant Euphrosynon because it gave a feeling of well being when the leaves or stems were put into wine or were eaten in salads. The leaves and stems compounded with a little lemon juice and added to a glass of white wine make a sustaining summer drink. They impart a cool cucumber-like flavour to cider and Pimms No. 1 and give the drinker an uplift when tired at the end of a long hot day.

There were plants able to effect a cure for almost every ailment and many to make appetising summer and winter drinks ('teas') before the introduction of China and Indian teas. There were plants to include in winter and summer salads and to serve with fish and game; as vegetables; and to make into sauces; plants such as lamb's lettuce which came early into leaf and so was highly thought of by countrymen during April and May when there were few other vegetables available; and fennel, which makes the best of all sauces to serve with mackerel and eel, whilst the stems were braised to serve with meats.

During the Tudor period many plants came to be appreciated for the pleasing scents they released when dry and were made into

2

pot pourris and sweet bags, scented washing waters and talcum powders. Roots and seeds were used, as well as flowers and leaves, for culinary and medicinal purposes. There were certain plants such as yellow loosestrife, which when hung up in a room would keep it free from flies in summer and others, such as wormwood and feverfew, which when placed amongst clothes and vestments were moth deterrents. Yet others such as the red rose, lavender and rosemary, which are believed to have come with the Romans 2000 years ago, were sweetly scented and these were also placed amongst clothes and bedding to impart their pleasing perfume rather than to keep away moths. Each of these plants were known as herbs which the dictionary defines as 'plants useful to man' and they were indeed in daily use from countryside and garden until the middle of the nineteenth century, when the Industrial Revolution took the population away from the countryside and from their gardens, to work in the mills and factories. Synthetic perfumes and man-made medicines soon took the place of these long-appreciated plants, though often they had unpleasant side effects as well as being more expensive to obtain.

Today, it is once again recognised that many herbs really are as efficient as they were once believed to be and are now being widely used in cosmetics (and in 'fringe' medicine); while cheaper continental travel has brought home to those who appreciate good food that the modern diet can be greatly improved by the inclusion of those same herbs which were appreciated in mediaeval times while others, included in salads, will greatly improve health. Herbs are some of the most important of all plants and our knowledge of them and of their culture will add greatly to the quality of our lives. As large a selection as possible should be grown in every garden for herbs can be used all the year round.

Laurel

The History of Herbs

The Roman invasion, 2000 years ago, saw the introduction into Britain of many herbs which were previously unknown. With the Romans' love of good living, they brought with them plants of southern Europe which have continued to enhance our standard of living. The Romans appreciated not only those plants which were grown to provide for their culinary and medicinal requirements but also for their well being. In their hot spring baths they placed the leaves of bay laurel and rosemary, to relieve their weary bodies after battle or a long march and to give pleasure as they released their delicate fragrance. In emulation of their women who garlanded themselves with scented flowers and leaves (as a substitute for perfume which was scarce and expensive), Roman generals took to self praise, crowning themselves with bay laurel when returning from victorious campaigns, hence the 'sweet bay' obtained its botanical name *Laurus nobilis* from the latin *laudare* (to praise) while 'bay' is from the Anglo-Saxon word meaning 'chaplet' or 'crown'. Roman women, and the men too, washed themselves in water made from saffron and red roses, the flowers of *Rosa gallica*, which they introduced into Britain from Gaul in northern France, an area they occupied before their invasion of Britain. With the dried petals of the red rose, which retains its scent when dry better than any other rose, and the flowers of lavender, they filled cushions and pillows to rest upon and they also included the dried leaves of bay and other sweet scented plants, while in the houses of the patricians, aromatics burnt continuously in a bronze censer, suspended from the raftered roof by chains. No meal was served unless accompanied by scented flowers and leaves and scented waters. Saffron and rose water was sprinkled over the guests as they sat down to dine, while servants massaged the neck and shoulders with fragrant oils. At the games, scented woods were burnt on altars and in lamps, placed at intervals around the arena, to counteract the oppressive heat and the unpleasant smells of those who attended.

Early uses of herbs

Many of the plants which had been introduced by the Romans were lost soon after their departure, due to lack of knowledge of their culture for they were plants of warmer regions and required well drained soils and open, sunny situations to grow well – very different conditions from those in our woodlands and hedgerows. But by the time of Alfred the Great, many of the herbs used in the more civilised parts of Europe had begun to reach Britain again, possibly brought back by those monks who travelled widely. St Boniface, a monk of Exeter living in the eighth century, mentioned receiving a letter from England while travelling in northern France, requesting him to bring back herbs that did not grow in Britain. In Bald's *Leechbook* of the tenth century, there are many herbal recipes, some of which were sent by the Patriarch of Jerusalem. Bald's *Leechbook* gives a prescription for sunburn using various plants, one being ivy which was to be boiled in butter or lard and applied to the sore parts, while for stimulating the growth of hair, one was advised to rub watercress on to the head, the juice of which would have the desired effect. Concoctions made from chamomile and wild lettuce were used to bathe the eyes and one was advised each morning upon rising, 'to look into cold water' which was to be highly recommended to give sparkle to the eyes.

For washing, the stems and leaves of the soapwort, to be found in hedgerows and on waste ground everywhere, were crushed and placed in warm water when the juice would make a thick lather.

Later the washing water was made fragrant by the addition of lavender or rose water.

Superstitions and herbs

Associated with the Anglo-Saxons' belief in witchcraft, was a certain amount of medical knowledge and in the *Lacnunga*, a ninth century leechbook, now in the British Museum, there is a recipe for a healing salve which could be recommended today as both soothing and healing. It says: 'take a handful of hammerwort (mugwort), one of maythe (chamomile), one of waybroad (plantain) and some water-dock roots (those which float), together with an eggshell of honey. Pound in butter and let him who would work up the salve, sing a mass over the worts before they are put together', perhaps to ensure that the preparation would not be skimped. The Anglo-Saxons recognised many superstitions connected with the herbs of the countryside. St John's wort was planted by the entrance to houses as it was believed to guard the occupants against spirits entering, and wormwood was planted to give protection against the shrew-mouse and dragon, both of which were thought to have poisonous bites. Angelica was thought able to guard the wearer from witches' spells and dill was used as an antidote to witches' potions and there was good reason to believe this for both plants soothe the lining of the stomach. This helps to counteract the poisonous effects of eating the berries of mistletoe and deadly nightshade which were included in witches' potions.

As people began to accept Christianity, many of the most beneficial herbs were given the name of a saint or took that of the Holy Family. Thus costmary was named in honour of the Blessed Virgin and St John's wort took its name from St John the Baptist for it is usually in bloom on the saint's feast-day, 24 June. The red sap, present in all parts of the plant, was thought to represent the saint's blood. Hyssop was the Holy Herb, taking its name from the Hebrew word *azob* (a holy plant) and it was used to strew over the floor of Westminster Abbey when it was first consecrated on 28 December 1065 and again, in more recent times, at the consecration of Westminster Cathedral. Tansy was named in honour of St Athanasius and the leaves were made into 'tansies', flat cakes which were eaten during Lent, in remembrance of the bitter herbs eaten at the Passover. Tansy cakes were served at the Coronation feast of James II and Mary of Modena, and Brand, in his popular *Antiquities* (1849) has described a north country custom when the young men of the village removed the buckles from the shoes of the girls on Easter Sunday and on the Monday the girls would do the same to the boys' shoes, redeeming them with forfeits of tansy cakes, this being one of the many delightful customs associated with herbs which had so many virtues that there was little wonder they enjoyed so great a popularity. It may reasonably be said that the people held them in great affection. Tansy is an example of the versatility of herbs. It was consumed in early summer salads for it was known to purify the blood. After putting the leaves and stems through the mixer, the juice, with a little orange juice added, makes a pleasant tonic drink at any time. Tansy 'tea' taken hot at night, will relieve a hard cough and the young leaves, finely chopped, make the best stuffing for a turkey. They make a delicious butter to use as a spread for cheese or tomato sandwiches and William Coles, in his *Art of Simpling*, said that if the leaves were soaked in buttermilk for ten days and it was applied to the face, it was soothing and healing and 'made the complexion very fair'. The plant had other uses too. Tusser, who published his *500 Points of Good Husbandry* in 1573, included it among the best of all plants for strewing over the floor of cottage and manor alike for when walked upon, it releases a powerful smell of camphor which is refreshing and it would keep the rooms free from flies and fleas. For the same reason, the dried leaves were placed in small muslin bags and put into beds. Like so many herbs, tansy was in daily use and so came to be appreciated, like most herbs, more than all other plants.

Several of our most popular herbs were possibly unintentionally introduced by the Normans, attached to the stone imported from Caen to build castles and abbeys and on which they are found growing to this day.

Dispensers of herbs

The monasteries were the first to make use of herbs medicinally for the monks were the only people who had knowledge of ailments and diseases and how to treat them. For about five hundred years after the Norman Conquest they acted as doctors to the population, administering their concoctions from the monasteries and as they travelled about the countryside. The herbarium, a separate garden attached to all monastic foundations was under the care of the sacristan, whose job it was to provide the monks with plants to make their cures. Later, the herb garden came to be attached to most churches to supply plants to strew over the floor and about the pews. In the accounts of the church of St Mary-at-Hill, London in 1483, there is an item to supply woodruff on St Barnabas Day, for as Gerard said, 'it does make fresh the place, to the delight and comfort of such as are therein'. When dry, it releases the pleasant smell of newly mown hay and for this reason it was collected from the countryside and used for strewing in even the poorest homes. Other herbs such as pennyroyal and water mint were used to freshen water, especially for those at sea, and these herbs used to be sold in the streets of London for this purpose.

There was also a considerable sale for the petals of red roses which were not only used to make scented water but when dry were put into sweet bags to place among clothes, while hot rose-water, sweetened with honey and taken at bedtime, brought relief to those suffering from asthma and bronchitis. A conserve of red roses is astringent and was given for dysentery and diarrhoea. There were herbs to bring relief to the pains of sciatica and rheumatism and others known to heal cuts and wounds. Parsley-Piert or 'Breakstone', which Nicholas Culpeper said 'grew in Hyde Park', was the most reliable remedy for breaking up stone or gravel in the kidneys. A handful of leaves in a pint of boiling water, sweetened with a little honey and taken daily, would, in Culpeper's words 'bring away gravel from the kidneys without pain'.

Before beer came to be made from hops which clarified it and imparted its distinctive flavour, ale was clarified with ground ivy and flavoured with meadowsweet and costmary which gave it a pleasant balsamic taste. Tonic drinks were made from lemon balm and wormwood, angelica and chamomile, dandelion and burdock. They were made in every home for the men to take with them when working in the woodlands and fields, since they were away

8

from home from dawn till dusk, working very long hours with the minimum of protective clothing.

Other herbs came to be appreciated for their many culinary uses, for stuffings when meat was scarce; to make into sauces to make fish more appetising; and to use as vegetables. As potatoes were not introduced into Europe until the sixteenth century, so all those plants which had edible roots to use in winter, were much appreciated. One of the most handsome of all our naturalised plants, the rampion, of the campanula family, was in demand in winter for its nourishing roots. Parkinson, who in 1629 dedicated his monumental work, the *Paradisus*, to Queen Henrietta Maria, said that rampion roots were 'boiled or braised and eaten with meats, or grated raw in a winter salad'. Writing soon after, John Evelyn said they were more nourishing than radishes (he meant winter radishes) and had 'a pleasant nutty flavour'. Countrymen would boil the roots of the annual Alexanders, a plant which may have come with the Romans, and use it as a substitute for parsnips, and they would blanch the stems of lovage by earthing soil around them and use them like celery, braising them or grating raw into salads. Though rarely used today, each of these plants would make a welcome and nourishing addition to our modern diet. The roots were lifted in autumn and stored in clamps of soil to use during winter, in the same way that we store turnips and other root crops today.

The old herbals

The first important book to be written about herbs in the Middle Ages was *De Proprietatibus Perum*. Its author was a Franciscan monk, Bartholomaeus Anglicus, believed to be a son of one of the Earls of Suffolk. He was educated at the University of Paris and the book was written in French. It was unknown in England until translated by a Cornishman, John de Trevisa, in 1398 and it was first printed in English by Wynken de Worde, Caxton's most famous apprentice. Of the seventeen volumes, one is entirely devoted to herbs and their properties and makes fascinating reading.

In 1440, the first practical work on gardening appeared, written in poetic style by John (the) Gardener; the manuscript is in the Library of Trinity College, Cambridge. Almost all the plants he mentioned had culinary value, including the cowslip, red rose, violet and paeony which we do not use today.

In the accounts of the monastery of Norwich for 1484 is an item, of 6 pence, paid to Robert the cook for 'herbs for the convent' and previously, there is an item of 2 shillings, paid for 'medicines of the gardener', presumably these being herbs used for medicinal purposes, and throughout the monastic rolls of the fifteenth century, there is mention of numerous sums, many of them quite considerable, being paid to the 'cellerer' for cutting and storing herbs to use during winter. This would be a most important job, for every aspect of life in the Middle Ages depended upon herbs and their culture, and their harvesting was of the greatest importance. It was as important to the people that the herbs were safely gathered in as it was for a good harvest, hence the phrase 'cut and dried' which means 'brought to a satisfactory conclusion'. In the monastic rolls there are payments shown for 'knives for cutting herbs' and these would be especially strong knives needed for cutting those herbs with woody stems, the shrubby herbs such as sage, thyme and rosemary.

The correct storing of herbs was of the utmost importance too, for enormous quantities were required for strewing over the monastery floors and later, in churches and houses, as well as for culinary and medicinal uses. The number of herbs then grown was considerable. As long ago as 1190, Alexander Neckham, when abbot of the monastery of Cirencester during the reign of Richard I, left us a detailed list of all the herbs which grew in the gardens there and among those used for culinary purposes were violets and red roses, alecost, fennel, coriander, sage, hyssop, dittany and rue, smallage and pellitory, lettuce (perhaps lamb's lettuce) and watercress, most of them still being in regular use.

Until the end of the fourteenth century, only the monasteries cultivated their own gardens but during the 'Black Death' when a third of the population of England perished from bubonic plague, only a small number of those who cultivated the open field strip system survived and these people took over the vacant lands and so became small tenant farmers. On these small areas of farmland, small homesteads arose where herbs and vegetables were grown and bees kept. Thus the first cottage gardens came into being and they provided the household with herbs to combat their daily ailments such as earache and coughs and to heal cuts, sprains and stiff joints, as well as providing a more varied diet.

As time went on and the people became more educated and began to read books, Herbals were written and have all manner of interesting recipes and of how to make *pot pourris* and sweet bags to put among clothes, and scented washing waters. From cowslips a delicious wine was made and from red roses a syrup called Melrosette, honey being the principal ingredient of these delicious concoctions. Anthony Askham gives the recipe for Melrosette in his *Little Herbal* which appeared early in the sixteenth century. It is to 'take fair purified honey and new red roses, the white ends clipped away. Chop the petals into a dish, add the honey and simmer.' And he adds, 'you shall know when it is ready, by the sweet odour and colour of red' and very delicious it is. It was taken in Tudor times to 'strengthen the heart' which red roses were supposed to do better than anything.

Tudor knot gardens

When the first of the Tudors came to the throne and the days were more settled following the Wars of the Roses, gardens were planted with scented flowers and leaves to distil, to make sweet waters for personal cleanliness and enjoyment, and all large houses had a still room. Balm and sage, marigold and tansy, rosemary and lavender were grown for this purpose. In 1527, appeared the first book devoted to the 'stilling of sweet waters'. It was written in German by Jerome of Brunswick and translated into English by Laurence Andrew, a copy of which is in the British Museum.

The beginning of the sixteenth century saw the first 'knot' gardens. These were gardens divided into numerous small beds of various shapes, often made in the form of a heart, each being enclosed or knotted together by a low hedge of box or of one of the low-growing, shrubby herbs which retained its leaves through winter. The beds were planted with other low-growing herbs and with cowslips and primroses, violets and pinks whose flowers were used in salads and to flavour wine and ale as Chaucer told us in The Tale of St Topaz, in the Prologue to *The Canterbury Tales*:

> ... and many a clove gillyflower,
> And nutmeg, to put in ale,
> Whether it be moist or stale....

The pink, with its clove-scented flowers, took its old name of gilly-flower from the French *girofleur* (a clove tree) and, along with other flowers and leaves to flavour drinks, it came to be grown in every tavern garden as well as in the knot beds of Tudor times.

During the reign of Edward VI, appeared the first part of Turner's *New Herbal*. Turner was a Morpeth man who became Dean of Wells and was a close friend of Bishops Latimer and Ridley. Physician to the Protector Somerset, Turner gives all manner of interesting uses for herbs and said that if southernwood was burnt in a room it would not only make it fragrant with its pungent smoke but would 'drive away serpents lurking in corners', meaning frogs and toads which often went into houses with earth or stone floors during warm, summer days, in search of cool, moist conditions. Of the marigold he showed his displeasure by saying: 'some use it to make their heyre yellow with the flowers, not being content with the natural colour which God hath given them'.

Soon after the publication of Turner's *New Herbal* (1551) appeared Thomas Tusser's *One Hundred Points of Good Husbandry* (1557) in which he gives advice on garden cultivation, how to grow and use herbs, on housekeeping and how to treat one's wife and servants. Tusser was born in Rivenhall in Essex in 1525 and was educated at Eton and Cambridge. Later, he took over a farm at Cattiwade and extended his earlier publication with *500 Points of Good Husbandry* which appeared in 1573. He died in 1580 and was buried in St Mildred's-in-the-Poultry. Among twenty plants he recommends for strewing, to release their refreshing perfume when trodden upon, he mentions basil and balm, lavender and hyssop, costmary and chamomile but surprisingly makes no mention of meadowsweet which was Queen Elizabeth's favourite strewing herb, though by that time her apartments would be covered with Eastern carpets and hangings. But so fond was the queen of having a regular supply of herbs for strewing always available that she appointed a lady to her household with a fixed salary with the sole purpose of having herbs in their season always in readiness.

In 1578, appeared Henry Lyte's *Herbal* and towards the end of the queen's reign John Gerard's most famous herbal was published. This appeared in 1596 and is the most interesting of all the old herbals, not least for the information he gives as to where many herbs can be found in and around London. Pennyroyal, he said, could be found at Mile End, and it was used in baths, 'to comfort the nerves and sinews'; and of yellow Archangel he told of finding it 'under the hedge on the left hand, as you go from the village of Hampstead ... and in the woods belonging to the Earl of Cobham, in Kent'. Of golden rod, which now plays little part in herbal remedies, he said it was sold in Bucklersbury for half a crown an ounce yet since it was found in Hampstead wood 'no man will give half a crown a hundredweight for it'.

In Gerard's time, Bucklersbury, situated between the Mansion House and Cheapside, was the centre of the herb and spice trade in the City. Sir Thomas More lived there before he moved to Chelsea and his daughter Margaret (Roper) was born there. Shakespeare knew it well for it was but a short walk from his lodgings to London Bridge and across to Bankside and the Globe Theatre. Throughout his plays, Shakespeare makes mention of herbs and spices. In *The Merry Wives of Windsor* Falstaff uses every device he knows to make an impression with Ford's wife but realising he is making little headway, he says, 'Come, I cannot cog, and say thou art this and that, like many of these lisping hawthorn buds, that come like women in men's apparel and smell like Bucklersbury in simpling time. I cannot, but I love thee; none but thee'.

13

Growing Herbs

In Shakespeare's day, herbs were known as 'simples' and at the height of the harvesting season Bucklersbury was redolent with the delicious scents as enormous quantities were sold from stalls and barrows every day of the week during August and September. The first people to deal in herbs and aromatics were the pepperers, a London guild mentioned in the Pipe Rolls as early as 1179. Soon after this date, they amalgamated with the spicers and each year paid a levy of herbs and spices to the king. One of their members was Odin the Spicer who was apothecary to Edward II's queen, Isabella of France who had the king murdered in Berkeley Castle in 1327. The pepperers and spicers, who had settled in Bucklersbury, dealt mainly in drugs for the medical profession and St Anthony was their patron saint. From the spicers, the trade in drugs eventually passed to the grocers and then to the apothecaries because, as their charter says, 'many unskilled and ignorant men do abide in our City of London which are not well instructed in the art and mystery of apothecarys and compound many unwholesome, hurtful and dangerous medicines and the same do sell . . . to the great peril of the lives of our subjects'. In 1617, James I met the Mayor and Corporation and told them he had granted their own charter 'from his own judgement for the health of the people'.

From Elizabethan times, herbs came to play an ever increasing part in the life of the people, for their personal cleanliness and their enjoyment. In all large houses, servants were employed for the sole purpose of fumigating rooms in readiness for the arrival of guests and in times of illness. Clothes were placed round open fires on which burnt fragrant woods and roots such as bay laurel and elecampane, for in those days clothes were rarely washed and there was no dry cleaning. Professional perfumers travelled the countryside to perfume those houses which did not employ servants to do so, according to Beaumont and Fletcher in *Wit Without Money*, 'selling rotten wood by the pound, which gentlemen burn by the ounce'.

Another pleasant practice was to rub the fragrant juice of certain herbs on to oak furniture and oak floors, and on to panelling and choir stalls and pews, to impart a polish and scent. Balm was widely used for the purpose, as Shakespeare tells us in Mistress Page's

14

Garter speech in *The Merry Wives of Windsor*. The pounded seeds and juice of sweet cecily was also used to impart a rich balsamic scent to furniture, so that all Elizabethan homes were sweetly scented and the scents of the furniture and strewing herbs were increased by the perfume of *pot pourris* (see the chapter on *Pot Pourris*, Sweet Bags and Scented Waters). The wealthy carried about with them pomanders made of silver or gold, fastened to a cord tied around the waist. The pomanders were filled with aromatic herbs and spices which released their scent through small holes. The poor carried with them oranges stuck with cloves or just a few sprays of tansy or rosemary to sniff whenever it was wished to counteract unpleasant smells.

The Doctrine of Signatures, formulated by the Italian inventor Della Porta and described in his *Phytognomonica* (1588), made it easier for herbalists to prescribe for the various ailments for as William Coles said 'God hath stamped upon plants ... particular signatures whereby a man may read in legible characters the use of them'. Thus the marigold was thought to cure jaundice and those plants with heart-shaped leaves were good for the heart.

Herbalists and physicians made use of the Doctrine of Signatures until well into the seventeenth century when Nicholas Culpeper, a staunch Roundhead, and always antagonistic towards the medical profession, put forward the theory that the planets should be given priority in determining choice of remedy. Culpeper was an astrologer as well as a herbalist and in 1652 appeared his book, *The English Physician*, which soon became 'the poor man's doctor'. By the end of the century, five editions had been printed and it was in continual use for two hundred years.

Many of the ideas put forward by the old herbalists may seem strange today but there was much truth in most of what they said. Two centuries after the publication of Culpeper's book, the Pasteur Institute of Paris discovered that the leaves of several herbs had powerful antiseptic qualities. For instance, it was found that the essential oils of cinnamon, angelica and thyme killed the micro-organisms of yellow fever in less than one hour and tubercle bacilli were destroyed or killed within twelve hours when exposed to the vapour of oil of lavender. Oil of thyme has several times the antiseptic strength of carbolic acid and during the Crimean War was used to spray the clothes of soldiers, to kill bacilli and keep them free from lice.

In his book, Culpeper also gives many reliable beauty aids. He suggests applying the juice of cucumbers and marigolds to the face to improve the complexion, and today both these are included in most face creams and there is a tendency to turn more and more to beauty preparations containing herbs. Yet by the time Culpeper's book appeared, Parkinson, who dedicated the best of all the herbals in his *Paradisus in Sole, Paradisi Terrestris* (1629) to Charles I's queen, Henrietta Maria had this to say, 'The former age of our great grandfathers had all the hot herbs both for their meats and medicines and therefore pursued themselves in long life and much health, but this delicate age of our's doth wholly refuse them'.

The opening of new trade routes brought with them the introduction of new plants while spices were imported from the East in ever increasing quantities to take the place of many plants native to our islands in culinary and medicinal practice. Citrus fruits replaced watercress and scurvy grass in the diet of the people and of those serving at sea, to combat scurvy with their vitamin C content, and hops were now being used to make beer whereas before it was made from malt and clarified by ground-ivy. Many other herbs were also used to impart to it their wholesome flavour. The movement from the country to the towns during the Industrial Revolution meant that the people lost the opportunity of collecting herbs or even to grow them and soon many valuable recipes handed down since earliest times were lost. Those working long hours in office, mill or factory needed instant remedies for their ailments and had little time for the old-fashioned ways of alleviating pain. A visit to the chemist who soon replaced the herbalist of village life was easier than making up herbal remedies.

Today, however, herbs are again in demand for it is realised that in many cases, their valuable medicinal qualities have been scientifically confirmed and they contribute fully to a healthy diet and to our appreciation of good food. What is more, herbs leave behind no unpleasant side effects that have come to be experienced when taking many of those pills and tablets prescribed today. A few people may be allergic to some herbs but this is rare.

Fennel

The Herb Garden

Herbs are all-purpose plants for besides their many uses, there is the wide variety of colour and form of their foliage to delight the eye which is an additional bonus to their many useful qualities and which creates interest wherever they are growing. Their foliage colours range from the almost pure silver of several of the achilleas and artemisias to the silver-green foliage of the lavenders and the silver-grey of cotton lavender. These herbs have foliage which is equally diverse in its beauty of form. The low growing artemisia Moonshine is made up of multitudes of leaves which have the appearance of tiny Prince of Wales feathers which when pressed release a deliciously pungent scent, while the leaves of the cotton lavender are like woolly lamb's tails though each is no more than $\frac{1}{2}$ in (1 cm) long. In contrast, the leaves of angelica measure at least 2 ft (60 cm) across and are divided into decurrent segments, while the silvery green leaves of mullein are broadly lanceolate, those near the base measuring about 8 in (20 cm) across and are often 12 in (30 cm) long.

The beautiful silver colour of the foliage of many herbs is because their leaves are covered in multitudes of tiny hairs and the closer they are together, the more silvered is the appearance of the leaves. With several herbs, and wormwood is an example, the hairs are longer than usual, like long silken threads which become entangled, while with mullein, the leaves are thick and downy. Indeed, the plant takes its name from the French, *molle* (soft) and, in olden days, parents would put the fresh leaves into their children's shoes to protect their feet against the roughly surfaced roads. Mullein is so densely covered in white hairs that its botanical name *verbascum* is from the Latin, *barbascum*, bearded, which gives rise to the occupation of barber. Even the filaments of the flowers are covered with white hairs.

The beauty of herbs

All the hairy herbs are native of the warmer parts of Europe, of the Mediterranean and southern Europe, of northern Africa and the Near East where they grow on barren rocks, exposed to the intense heat of the sun for long hours each day. The hairs help to prevent the too rapid transpiration of moisture, as with the pelargoniums of South Africa amongst which are many scented, leaf species and varieties. In the same way that hairs give the plants protection, so those plants with finely divided leaves are able to survive high temperatures for the loss of moisture in dry weather is very small. Of these plants, and southernwood and fennel are popular examples, both being native of southern Europe and the Mediterranean, their beauty lies in the delicate fern-like tracery of their leaves with fennel taking on a blue-green colour when in full leaf. Another herb of similar colouring is rue, the variety Jackman's Blue having the bluest foliage of any plant, while the leaves are divided into numerous segments which makes the rues among the most beautiful of all plants.

There are also those herbs which have golden leaves. There is the golden leaved thyme and golden sage, *Salvia officinalis aurea*, while there is a handsome golden-leaf variety of the Pot marjoram, *Origanum onites* which Parkinson described in the *Paradisus* (1629). These plants provide striking contrast to the blue leaved rues and to those herbs with dark green foliage. Among the darkest are rosemary, which also has tiny leaves and is native of the Mediterranean regions, and Roman wormwood, native of the same part of Europe, both being among the most handsome plants of the herb garden.

Herbs of the colder regions, of the British Isles and northern Europe usually have an entire surface, not broken up into finely divided segments like those of warmer climes yet many are covered in long hairs, if not densely so for the hairs give protection from the cold. Examples are ground ivy and mallow. The leaves are often attractively heart-shaped and usually are lobed or have serrated edges which add to their interest while with many, the leaves are deeply channelled or grooved. This allows rain water to drain away as quickly as possible for these herbs grow in areas of high rainfall. It also allows moisture to reach the plants' roots during dry weather with the minimum of evaporation for these herbs are accustomed to surviving in a cold, moist climate. Examples are elecampane and the primrose and cowslip.

Some herbs have a beauty when in bloom exceeding all other plants and, for this alone, are worthy of a place in any flower border. Some are perennial, some are annual plants and all are of easy culture. Our native elecampane which has violet-scented roots, bears the largest flowers of all our native plants, measuring 3 in (7·5 cm) or more across and resembling golden-yellow single chrysanthemums, while the deeply wrinkled leaves are more than 12 in (30 cm) long. Growing 5–6 ft (1·5 m) tall, it is a giant of a plant and when in bloom is of the greatest beauty. It should take its place at the back of a border and with it, plant the equally handsome mullein which bears tall, elegant spikes of biscuit-yellow flowers and has silver foliage. It will grow 6–7 ft (2 m) tall and is biennial, usually seeding itself. To the front of them, plant rampion whose flowers of purple or white are the largest of the bellflowers or campanulas and are borne in large erect spikes or panicles.

Another herb which is handsome in bloom is the monarda or bergamot, so called from the resemblance of the scent of its leaves to that of the Bergamot orange of Italy. It is one of the few herbs to reach us from the new world and it bears its pink, red or white flowers in whorls. From its leaves a delicious 'tea' is made, to be drunk hot or ice cold in summer, and the leaves are also used in *pot pourris*. Hyssop is another herb which is most attractive when in bloom, likewise the yellow Gentian, which bears interesting yellow flowers spotted with brown or black, while yellow loosestrife bears its golden-yellow flowers in large cymes from the axils of the leaves. Each of these plants, and there are others, will bring distinction to the flower border and there are those, of more shrubby habit, which are at home in the shrub border. These include the rosemary and lavender, both handsome in bloom and the sages, especially the red-stemmed variety, purpurea, its leaves also being splashed with purple or red, and the golden-leaved aurea.

Lavender, with its flower spikes of purple or blue and much visited by butterflies and bees, is well known to all lovers of pleasing perfumes but the flowers of rosemary, of a lovely ethereal blue, also have a beauty all their own. What is more, they appear early in spring when few other flowers are open, and at this time are a particular attraction for bees. They can be included in salads and with them, those of cowslips and primroses which also open at this time.

In the shrub border may also be planted the Red Rose of Lancaster, *Rosa gallica*, the Apothecary's rose, so called because the dried petals which retain their scent longer than all other roses, were once sold by the pound at most apothecaries' shops, to use medicinally and in *pot pourris* and sweet bags. Plant small groups of two or three about the shrub border for when in bloom, in mid-summer, the blood red flowers are seen to advantage against the silver-greys of lavender and the achilleas and the blue-green of the rues. Also attractive when in bloom is the cotton lavender, its multitudes of bright yellow buttons appearing above the silver-grey foliage; but though the foliage has a pungent appetising smell, that of the flowers is most unpleasant, in spite of which it should be used about the herb garden as much as possible.

All of these shrubby herbs are plants of great hardiness although native of the Mediterranean regions and so too are those of the flower border. Very few herbs are tender in Britain and northern Europe and of these, basil which is native of India is the least hardy while marjoram and pineapple sage will not usually survive a severe winter. But most other perennial herbs present no trouble in this respect provided they are given a well drained soil and an open, sunny situation.

Few herbs are tolerant of shade, perhaps only the mints and the closely related ground ivy and there are few which can tolerate a wet soil. Here again, the mints and ground ivy are among those that will survive such conditions and yellow loosestrife, monarda and to a lesser extent, the cowslip and primrose, marshmallow and meadowsweet. The natural terrain of the herbs of southern Europe and the Mediterranean is rocky ground of a calcareous nature and these are the conditions necessary to bring out the full strength of the essential oil in their leaves for which sunlight is also a necessity. Away from the sun, plants are never as fragrant. Ground which is shaded by buildings or by overhanging trees, or where it slopes towards the north, will never grow good herbs. An open, sunny position is therefore the first essential when making a herb garden.

Cultural requirements

Herbs will not grow well in the acid soil of town gardens created by the continual deposits of soot and sulphur from factory chimneys. Herbs do not need rich soil, in fact manure and artificial fertilisers are harmful to them apart from a little decayed manure which may be given as an occasional top dressing. Before planting herbs, give the ground a liberal dressing of hydrated lime or mortar which is obtainable from old buildings when being demolished in areas of town clearance. If the soil is heavy, and this will not be conducive to growing good herbs, dress the ground with unhydrated lime obtainable from a builder's merchant. This is applied in autumn and is dug in while the soil is still dry. With the winter rains, the lime will disintegrate with a violent reaction, causing the clay particles of the soil to break up. Winter frosts and winds will complete the breaking down of the soil so that it can be brought to a fine tilth ready for planting in spring.

Also a help in bringing clay soil into a suitable condition is Aerosil, a product of British Gypsum Limited of Kingston-on-Soar. If applied when the soil is reasonably dry, it will help to break down the colloid matter of a heavy soil, yet will bind a sandy soil, bringing it into better condition. It is expensive to use but will also provide mineral salts of magnesium and calcium which the plants will appreciate.

A heavy soil can be brought into suitable condition for herbs by incorporating some drainage materials such as crushed brick, shingle and garden compost but for herbs, a light friable loam, especially of a calcareous nature, will be most suitable and apart from keeping it free from weeds, will require no further attention. Good drainage is more important than plant food. This is one of the most important factors when considering what plants to grow in the garden for, as most organic manures are difficult to obtain and artificials are expensive to buy, any plants able to grow well without either are to be recommended. Given a well drained soil and an open situation, herbs are among the easiest of plants to grow. They require no special diet apart from some lime or mortar and little attention as to their watering, surviving long periods of drought so that they will come to no harm if one is away from home for several weeks at a time even during mid-summer. They are labour saving plants in this respect and also in their culture, requiring little by way of staking, this being necessary for only a few of the taller growing plants and perhaps for some annuals being grown for seed. All the plants require is care with their harvesting, whether it is their seeds, flowers, or leaves and this is usually done in early autumn, when much of the garden work such as mowing grass and clipping hedges is becoming less urgent.

Propagating herbs

Herbs are propagated by root division from cuttings which is done for those plants of shrubby or woody habit or by sowing seed. Annual and biennial herbs are raised from seed sown in late summer (if treating the plants as biennial) or in spring (for annuals) but many perennials are also propagated in this way and although taking longer to reach maturity, this is the cheapest way of obtaining a stock. Specialist growers, however, can supply many of the rare herbs which are not available from seed; plants such as rue, Jackman's Blue which must be propagated by vegetative methods (cuttings) to maintain the true stock. With some perennial herbs grown from seed there is some variation of quality and type; with others this is not so. (Methods of propagation are given under each herb throughout this book.)

Herbs in the garden

The smallest of gardens can be made to grow a wide selection of herbs, enough to supply the kitchen with all that is needed the whole year round, and for medicinal purposes too. Others will be used for 'teas' and to flavour drinks and others for *pot pourris* and sweet bags, washing waters and as moth deterrents. There are at least one hundred 'useful plants', which, if grown in the garden, will be to hand whenever required. With their various leaf colours and forms, a herb garden is always an attraction quite apart from the many uses the plants can be put to and it is a most pleasant occupation to grow herbs, to make up into sweet bags and *pot pourri* mixtures. Suitable herbs can be grown in the garden or allotment for this purpose and after correctly drying, are blended and then placed in pretty bags which may be made up from pieces of unwanted material. They have a ready appeal the whole year round, especially before Christmas to give as presents but they also make attractive birthday and mothers' day gifts and so there is no particular season when they are most in demand.

A herb garden can be made at one end of the garden or in a corner, provided it receives the maximum amount of sunshine. If surrounded by a hedge of one of the taller growing lavenders or rosemary, these plants, as well as being useful, will protect other herbs from cold winds. Or erect a screen of rustic fencing posts and plant the deliciously scented, thornless rose, Zephirine Drouhin, at 6 ft (about 2 m) intervals, tying in the long whippy stems as they increase in length, when they will completely cover a screen 6 ft (about 2 m) high in two years. The roses appear early in June and continue until well into autumn and are of a lovely shade of silvery pink. They will scent a large garden with their fragrance and associate to perfection with herbs.

When erecting the screen, allow a 3 ft (90 cm) space for entry. This may be through a rustic arch over which the roses can be trained. Strong galvanised wires at intervals of about 15 in (38 cm) and held in place by wooden stakes or rustic posts driven well into the ground at 6 ft (about 2 m) intervals will be an alternative

23

way of enclosing the herb garden, the roses being trained and tied to the wires which will soon be hidden. An additional attraction will be to plant a row of dwarf lavender between the posts and the purple flowers will make a most attractive picture when in bloom with the deep pink of the roses during the three mid-summer months, and both the lavender and the roses can be used in *pot pourris*. A herb garden can be enclosed in this way and if possible it should cover an area of not less than 20 ft (6 m) square where a large number of herbs of every size, shape and colour can be grown.

One of the attractions of gardening with herbs is that they can be planted together, herbs of all sizes and shapes in the same bed, provided each is given sufficient room to develop and those of more compact habit are not deprived of sunlight by taller growing herbs. In the small herb garden at Sissinghurst Castle in Kent, there are four square beds surrounded with a narrow path of paving stones and enclosed by yew hedges and each bed contains herbs of every size and colour. The appearance is one of great charm as they grow over the paths and each bed is comprised of herbs which have a different purpose. One is filled with culinary herbs; another with herbs for making 'teas' and to flavour drinks; another is planted with herbs for simple medicinal remedies; another with herbs suitable to make *pot pourris*, sweet bags and scented waters. The taller growing plants are placed at or near the centre of each bed and those of dwarf or trailing habit near the edges so that they can grow over the stones. Each bed contains a few clumps of pinks which are used in *pot pourris* although they are not now used to flavour drinks as they were in Chaucer's day, and a plant or two of red roses (*Rosa gallica*) to give a generous splash of colour among the silver and grey foliage of the herbs and one can never have too many red roses to include in *pot pourris* and to make scented waters. Plant the silver artemisias with the blue-green rues, the golden sage with the dark green wormwoods, those which bear yellow flowers with the purples and blues, when the whole garden will be like a patchwork quilt, each herb being quite distinct from another yet each blending perfectly one with another and no other garden plants are able to achieve quite such harmony.

Those herbs of shrubby habit can be planted with other shrubs to make a shrub border. Most of these herbs, which include the lavenders and rosemary, sages and thymes, possess great hardiness although most are native of southern Europe. Once planted, they need little attention for they will be kept in bounds by constantly using them. The shrubby herbs grow best in a calcareous soil but ordinary loam suits them well provided it is not lacking in lime. The soil must have an alkaline reaction, not acid.

A shrub border can be mostly devoted to herbs, but some of the scented shrub roses suitable for *pot pourris* and certain other shrubs bearing fragrant flowers can be planted too to add colour and interest. If the shrubs are planted in well cleaned ground, they will need little attention through the years apart from an occasional dressing with lime in autumn and a top dressing of decayed manure in spring. The shrubby herbs are tolerant of dry conditions and more than other herbs, require a well drained soil and an open, sunny situation. They will not tolerate shade nor a cold northerly position.

Those herbs of herbaceous habit and which are hardy perennials may be planted in a border to themselves or with other perennials of similar habit. The plants will die down in autumn after flowering, when the border should be cleared of top growth and the ground around the plants forked over, at the same time incorporating materials from the compost heap or decayed manure, used hops or old mushroom bed compost as these herbs require some humus in the soil. Early in spring, the plants will begin to grow again and for them to be seen in the fullness of their beauty, those of taller habit should be given support as they make growth.

As with all borders, set the taller plants to the back, remembering that some herbs will grow 6–7 ft (2 m) tall, with those of more compact habit in front of them and planting the most dwarf to the front of the border. A border may be of any length and could be made on one side of the herb garden with a shrub border opposite, the two being separated by a broad path of crazy paving or old bricks with prostrate herbs planted here and there in openings left between the stones. The borders should be not less than 6 ft (say 2 m) wide so that some of the herbs can be set out in groups of two or three which will supply the house with plenty of leaves and flowers. Some herbs have many uses and can be used both fresh and when dry, and so are in constant use throughout the year.

Many of the herbaceous herbs are among the most attractive plants to the garden and these include the monarda which is used in *pot pourris* and makes a delicious summer 'tea'; hyssop, its pink or purple flowers beloved of bees; fennel with its leaves of delicate tracery and of blue-green colouring; meadowsweet with its creamy-white spiraea-like flower heads and fragrant foliage of darkest green; angelica and balm and many others. All of them are hardy and are not particular as to soil but whereas the shrubby herbs prefer a well drained sandy soil containing some lime or mortar, those herbs of herbaceous habit require a soil containing humus to retain summer moisture, otherwise they will not make as much growth as they should do. They are readily propagated by root division between November and March when the soil is in suitable condition.

A number of annual plants such as marigolds and clary, which are also given biennial treatment, may be included in the herb border but some annuals and biennials are best grown in the vegetable garden or by themselves for they are grown for seed and require a poor, dry soil and plenty of sunshine.

There are also a number of herbs apart from the handsome elecampane and rampion, grown for their roots and here, too, they are best confined to the vegetable garden where they may be lifted for use or for drying and storing without disturbing other plants growing nearby. The root herbs require a soil well enriched with humus to retain summer moisture and a deeply worked soil, conditions which are exactly the opposite for those grown for seed. Where the garden is very small, a delightful herb garden in miniature can be made perhaps in the centre of a lawn, cutting out a circle of turf of not less than 6 ft (say 2 m) diameter but if the lawn is large, then make the circle larger to keep it in proportion and at the centre may be placed a stone bird bath or sundial. Or make the circular garden in a sunny corner if the lawn is required for games.

The garden should be made to resemble an old cartwheel, using chives perhaps, to represent the spokes and to divide the garden into segments, each of which will be planted with a different herb of compact habit. For the rim, the upright thymes could be used, alternating the dark green leaved with the gold leaf; or use cotton lavender and keep it clipped back to about 6 in (15 cm) tall. It will make a dense circular hedge if planted about 12 in (30 cm) apart and will protect the other plants from cold winds.

Each section of the wheel (and there should be eight) is then planted with one of the more compact herbs, using those that will be of the greatest use in the kitchen. One or more sections could be planted with the thymes, another with pot marjoram, another with mint and so on, while parsley could be sown at the centre for the hub, or this too might be of chives which are in constant use for flavouring, and parsley sown in one of the segments.

Herbs in the window box

Herbs in the window box

Many of the more compact herbs may also be planted in a window box. This may be constructed of wood and fixed either inside or outside a sunny window. A box planted with herbs will be both interesting and useful if grown in the kitchen window for the plants will remain green all the year however severe the weather is outside. The box could be planted with several of the thymes, including the orange-scented *T. fragrantissimus* and with several clumps of chives, and with parsley, sown in small pots and transferred with the soil ball intact, to the window box. The useful marjorams can be grown indoors, and sweet basil which is happier when growing in this way, protected from frost and cold winds; or grow it in pots in a sunny window.

27

For outdoor boxes, and these may be placed on a terrace or verandah, for the herbs to be used all year, plant the hardier herbs such as parsley and thyme; chives and other bunch onions; winter savory, so called because it is perennial and can be used all year whereas summer savory is available only in summer; and perhaps sage which can be kept low and bushy if constantly used.

A window box is best constructed of seasoned timber and should be made to the correct width of a window. Before filling the box it must be made secure for it has to take a considerable weight of soil, and it must be fixed where it can be easily attended either from inside or outside for watering the plants and for cutting them for kitchen use. Herbs require a friable compost, made up of decayed turf loam to which is incorporated some mortar or lime and a little coarse sand for drainage. The box should contain a few holes to allow surplus moisture to drain away. Cover them with 'crocks' or pieces of brick to prevent the holes being choked with compost or the compost from falling through the holes if it is dry. Then fill the boxes almost to the top when the compost will soon settle down to just below the top of the box and this will allow for watering without the compost splashing over the sides. But herbs need the minimum of moisture and will usually obtain sufficient from the rains.

Wherever it is sited, the box must be where the herbs will receive plenty of sunlight and they must be sheltered from cold winds to give of their best. The boxes are best made up in spring.

Those herbs of creeping habit, the mountain thymes and the Corsican thyme, may be planted between old bricks or crazy paving stones used to make a path. These plants will quickly spread over the stones and do not mind being walked upon. They retain their foliage all year and are especially attractive when in bloom, the mountain thymes presenting a carpet-like appearance during July and August for there are a number of varieties which bear flowers of vivid colouring. The paving plants require a well drained soil and an open, sunny situation and may also be used to make a fragrant 'lawn'.

Harvesting and drying herbs

Herbs present few difficulties in their growing but their harvesting and drying calls for the greatest care. Those grown for their seeds, which will ripen in Britain only in a year of above average sunshine and in the drier Essex and East Anglia, are mostly annual or biennial plants, preferably sown the previous year for this gives them more time to develop and to ripen. The seeds are removed early in autumn, just as the capsules begin to open. If left too long, much of the seed will be lost but if harvested too early, the seed will not have ripened fully and will have little flavour, neither will they dry correctly. They should be harvested on a dry day, cutting off the heads and, with care, placing them in boxes lined with paper. Each box should be named, and removed without delay to a dry, airy room (an attic is ideal). Here the seed heads should be carefully spread out on a table or bench which has been lined with white paper so that every seed which falls from the capsules can be saved. After about a month, when the seeds will have become quite dry and will have turned deep brown or black, they are removed from the capsules and placed in muslin bags or jars, each being clearly named before they are placed in a dry cupboard to use when required.

Herbs can be used fresh, when the leaves and 'tops' are removed from the plants or they can be dried for winter use. This is usually done for those herbs which die back in late autumn or if growing in an exposed garden, when they might lose their leaves in a severe winter. Herbs must be dried correctly or they will become mildewed and will lose their fragrance and flavour and have little or no value. With some herbs, two cuttings are made, the first towards the end of June which is usually a time of dry, sunny weather which makes their drying easy, and again in autumn, towards the end of September.

All herbs are at their best and are most potent following a period of hot, dry weather and, if this has occurred, they must be harvested without delay, before the essential oil in the leaves is lost. In a difficult year, in which sunshine and rain alternate almost daily, select a dry day for the harvesting and after cutting the plants well back, place the stems in deep boxes and remove to a dry, airy room without delay. Spread out the stems, which will have been removed with a sharp knife or secateurs, on a table covered with sheets of clean brown paper and turn them every two or three days so that all the leaves will dry as quickly and as evenly as possible; or place them on a drying rack. This is made of builder's laths and is fixed to a wall of a shed or attic. If more than one rack is required, they are fixed to the wall at intervals of about 16 in (40 cm) one above another from floor to ceiling. Each rack should be about 2 ft (60 cm) wide with the laths 2 in (5 cm) apart. This will allow a free circulation of air to reach the herbs and, if the racks are lined with clean hessian canvas, this will prevent the leaves from falling through, yet will not deprive them of air. When placing the herbs on the racks, keep them separate from each other for they will complete their drying at different times, depending on the day they were harvested, whether it was dry and sunny or dull which will determine the amount of moisture in the leaves. Those plants with thick leaves take longer to dry than those with less thick or finely divided leaves. Some herbs, too, will be ready to harvest before others.

The leaves are quite dry if they crackle when touched. They are then removed from the stems by rubbing between the hands. The stems are discarded (though not lavender stems which can be burnt like incense in the home) and the leaves placed into small boxes, preferably of wood or cardboard but never of tin which 'sweats' during changes of temperature and will cause the herbs to become covered with mildew. Remember to name the contents of each box and store them in a dry, airy room or cupboard.

Another way of keeping herbs through winter is to string them up in a dry room, but with this method leaves are often lost as they dry and often part from the stems and become covered with dust. But where storage facilities are absent, this is a simple way to keep the herbs through winter. Alternatively, the airing cupboard can be used for drying herbs, leaving the door slightly open to allow any moisture to escape and removing clothes and linen until the herbs are quite dry. The herbs will leave behind a pleasant aroma which will permeate the clothes.

The most difficult of all herbs to dry is parsley with its thick crinkled leaves. The best method is to place it in a low oven, spreading out the fronds and turning them every hour. A temperature of 80°–100°F (27°–36°C) is necessary and it may take several days to complete the drying which should be done during daytime perhaps when the oven is used for other purposes.

Propagating herbs

No great expense will be necessary in buying equipment for herb growing but a small garden frame will be useful when raising plants from seed and for striking cuttings, while young plants can be grown on during winter in small pots, protected from hard frost or excess moisture. Most herbs are perfectly hardy once they have become established, those of shrubby habit protecting themselves and each other by their dense foliage but when the plants are small they need protection from cold winds and hard frost, and from winter moisture if the soil is not too well drained. A frame will do just that and may be simply constructed from 8 in (20 cm) boards cut to the size of a frame light and held in place by strong pegs driven into the ground. The frame light can be glazed or made from heavy gauge plastic material fastened to the wooden frame. During windy weather, the light(s) is held in place by wires stretched across and fastened to the sides of the frame.

Herbs from seed

Many herbs can be raised from seed sown at any time between early March (if a frame is available) and September. Biennials can be sown in July, and wintered in a frame, to be planted out in spring and this is done in the colder parts of Britain where the plants might perish if sown outdoors. In the south and west, seeds are sown in drills outdoors and, if necessary, covered with cloches during winter.

The seeds are sown in pots or boxes containing the John Innes compost, obtainable from nurserymen or garden shops. It is composed of:

> 2 parts sterilised loam
> 1 part peat
> 1 part sand

$\frac{1}{2}$ oz (14 g) superphosphate of lime
$\frac{3}{4}$ oz (21 g) ground limestone

The compost should be freshly prepared for the superphosphate, necessary to promote root activity, soon loses strength, while the sterilised loam may have become re-contaminated with weed seeds and disease spores if left for several weeks before using.

If the compost is unobtainable, use sterilised loam and add the superphosphate. Soil in which seeds are being sown should always be sterilised to ensure that there are no disease spores present which would cause the seedlings to damp off or die back, while weed seeds which would be in competition with the herb seeds, will be eliminated at the same time.

Sow the seeds thinly, so that there is no overcrowding to cause the young plants to grow spindly, and just cover with compost. Then water in and place in a frame which should be kept closed until germination is complete. Water with care, keeping the compost nicely moist but not wet. In summer, shade the seedlings from the direct rays of the sun when the seed has germinated. The seedlings should then be given fresh air by raising the frame light and they must be transplanted to small pots or boxes of similar compost when large enough to handle. The seedlings may be moved to Vacapots which are thin-walled plastic containers divided into twenty-four detachable units, each being 2 in (5 cm) square and 2 in (5 cm) deep. If the seedlings are transplanted towards the end of summer, they are grown on in the Vacapots all winter and planted out in spring or the trays are sold to garden shops or chain stores for, at this time, herbs are always in demand.

Propagation by root division

Hardy herbaceous herbs are propagated by lifting and dividing the plants in autumn or spring and they require no winter protection but those herbs of a shrubby nature such as lavender and rosemary, sage and thyme, although they come readily from seed, are usually propagated from cuttings of the young woody stems. These are removed late in summer when about 4 in (10 cm) long, treated with hormone powder to persuade them to root more quickly and are inserted in pots or boxes of sandy compost, preferably in a frame which will enable a moist atmosphere to be maintained. This will prevent excessive transpiration from the leaves and so will help the cutting to root more quickly. Perennial herbs raised from seed should be given protection either by covering the seed boxes with a sheet of glass or with plastic to accelerate germination or by giving them the protection of a frame, for they take considerably longer to germinate than annuals or biennials which are usually sown outdoors.

A quantity of plastic or earthenware pots will be required for growing on the rooted cuttings, but 'Root o' Pots', made of best Irish peat moss and wood fibre, or 'Jiffy Pots', which are compressed pots made of a special growing medium, are excellent in every way for the plants' roots will grow into the pots and they can be planted out still in the pots. Peat pots also take up and hold more moisture than plastic pots and so the plants require less attention with watering.

For planting, a trowel and a rake are needed to break down the soil and also to make seed drills with the back. The drills are required for sowing seeds of annuals and biennials, which are best sown where they are to mature, for some will not transplant well and where transplanting must be done, this will cause a check in growth which may result in the seeds failing to ripen correctly in a poor year.

For preparing the soil, a spade and a fork are necessary tools and, where the garden is of reasonable size, a barrow will be an asset. This may be used for moving compost for top dressing and also, after lining the barrow with clean sacking, to place in herbs which are being harvested.

Other tools needed will be a hoe to stir the soil between the plants, to suppress weeds and to aerate the soil after the winter rains and snow, and a pair of efficient secateurs to cut the shrubby herbs for harvesting and to prune them if necessary.

Sage   *Red Rose*   *Germander*

Herbs for a Shrub Border

Among the most lasting and useful of all herbs are those of woody or shrub-like habit which retain their foliage during winter and grow into dense bushes, providing their own protection from frost and cold winds. Some, like southernwood (which can lose its leaves in a cold winter), lavender and rosemary will eventually grow to 3–4 ft (1 m) across and to about the same in height. Rosemary, growing against a wall, will reach 6–7 ft (2 m). They can accompany other shrubs to make a shrub border and they grow best in a dry, sandy soil of a calcareous nature so if using other plants with them, plant only those requiring similar conditions and the choice is wide. These plants also require an open, sunny situation, none liking shade, and they will grow best where given protection from strong winds. Cold east winds tend to burn the foliage when the plants are young, while the stronger west winds may cause the woody stems to break off and spoil their appearance. Most of them, with the exception of bay laurel and pineapple sage, will withstand the severest weather, the winter of 1978–79 causing them little trouble except where the weight of snow caused damage to sage and lavender by breaking off the older branches. If the garden is exposed, erect interwoven fencing panels on the side of the prevailing wind or provide the newly planted shrubby herbs with shelter by placing round them during their first two winters, windbreaks made of sacking or canvas, held in place by stakes driven into the ground. These should be in position by the first days of December and remain so until the end of March. This will usually provide the plants with all the protection they need. As they grow older they will protect each other.

Even where growing the shrubby herbs with other herbs, it is advisable to give them some protection when newly planted for those herbs of the flower border will mostly die back in autumn and will give little winter protection to the others.

Of all herbs, those of a shrubby nature make a greater contribution to the garden than any others for their leaf colourings are unique. There is rue with its handsome leaf formation and its blue-green colouring, the variety Jackman's Blue having leaves of metallic blue which is unique among garden plants, while the variegated form has its leaves splashed with cream and gold. The artemisias are grey-leaved and here, too, several have leaves which resemble tropical ferns in their formation. The beautiful Silver Queen is an example. It grows 2 ft (60 cm) tall and has finely cut leaves which are so silvered as to appear covered with frost, while *Santolina incana*, 'Weston', a dwarf form of cotton lavender, has leaves like tiny lambs tails and of a lovely shade of silver-grey. The lavenders are grey-green, the white flowered *L. nana alba* being more grey than others and the common wormwood, has handsome, attractively lobed, dull green leaves covered with grey down. Southernwood has finely divided leaves of a paler and brighter grey-green. At the other end of the spectrum is rosemary, with its narrow leaves of dark forest green. It acts as a striking contrast to those with grey leaves and should be planted at the back of the shrub border, near the taller growing old English lavender.

Planting the border

When planting the shrub border, do so for contrasting foliage colours and also for the various heights, grouping the taller growing herbs at the back and those of dwarf habit such as the marjorams and thymes to the front. The lavenders of more compact habit can be planted towards the front with several groups of the

Apothecary's Rose, the Red Rose of Lancaster, at the centre for it grows about 2 ft (60 cm) tall, the same as tansy, rue and sage. The table at the end of the chapter (pp. 51–2) will give the various heights and chief uses of the shrub border herbs. They have many uses, culinary and medicinal as well as for making *pot pourris* and sweet waters, for hair rinses and skin tonics. When planting, allow them plenty of room to develop and give each plant the same space as it grows tall. Thus the more vigorous lavenders and rosemary should be planted about 4 ft (say 1·5 m) apart; those plants growing 2 ft (60 cm) tall should be planted 2 ft (60 cm) apart and those growing only half the height, may be planted 1 ft (30 cm) apart. If planted closer together, they will have grown into each other within two years and will deprive each other of sunlight and air, and where they touch will tend to die back. The best time to plant the shrubby herbs is in spring when, in the mild showery weather, they will get away to a good start but wait until all frost is out of the ground and it is in a friable condition.

Light, sandy soil is well drained and ideal for herbs. Otherwise, work in plenty of humus such as garden compost, decayed manure, used hops or leaf mould, together with some grit or shingle. Crushed brick is useful, so are the clearings from ditches which will contain decayed leaves and grit washed down from roads and waste ground. Above all, give the ground a liberal dressing of lime or mortar, obtainable where old buildings are being de-molished. Shrub herbs grow best in calcareous soils and, where mortar is not available, work in some crushed chalk or limestone. While most herbs grow better without manure, those of a shrubby nature will appreciate a small amount of well decayed farmyard manure, cow manure especially, dug in before planting and given every two years as a mulch, alternating with a mulch of limestone or mortar. This, together with regular attention to their pruning, will keep the plants healthy for many years, and they will become a permanent part of the garden.

Several herbs may also be grown as a hedge for they will stand clipping to keep them in shape if done regularly and in this way the plants will not accumulate a mass of old wood. The old English lavender and rosemary, planted 3–4 ft (1 m) apart will make an excellent hedge to surround a rose or herb garden, or to divide one part of the garden from another. The cotton lavender also makes an admirable hedge but as it grows about 2 ft (60 cm) tall it is best used to surround or edge the herb garden or border. Planted 20 in (50 cm) apart, it makes plenty of dense growth low down. It may be clipped in spring each year, like box which was once widely used for the same purpose but is very slow growing. A hedge of cotton lavender may be cut into any desired shape, rounded at the top, or square and provides a striking contrast to the other herbs with its neat grey-green foliage. It is particularly effective if red roses and scarlet geraniums are planted close to it. Clipped back each year, cotton lavender can be kept to 12 in (30 cm) tall but the marjorams which are also evergreen, are even more compact. It is the wild or common marjoram, *Origanum vulgare compactum*, and its golden leaf variety, *aureum*, that is perennial and used for a low hedge, often for knot gardens, for it grows 8 in (20 cm) tall and it too, can be clipped lightly into shape. With each of these herbs, the clippings and prunings can be dried and used in *pot pourris* and for other purposes.

The common marjoram, like the others described in this chapter, is a woody plant and is propagated from cuttings. These are removed in July or August when the new season's wood is half-ripe. The cuttings should be about 4 in (10 cm) long and should preferably be pulled away from the main stems with a 'heel' attached. Root them in pots or boxes or in a cold frame, in a sandy compost. By late autumn they should have rooted and are then moved to small pots containing a similar sandy compost and grown on until spring when they are planted out. All the shrubby herbs are propagated in like manner.

These herbs will require little pruning for their regular use will keep them trim. They should not, however, be allowed to form an excess of old wood and those bare older stems or those damaged by strong winds, should be removed near the base to allow the plant room to form fresh new shoots. This will keep them healthy over a long period of time.

If other shrubs are to be planted with them, these herbs associate well with the shrubby loniceras, especially *L. nitida*, Baggeson's Gold, which stays gold all winter and is particularly effective growing near rosemary. It provides wonderful shelter. The evergreen *Berberis darwinii* with its shiny holly-shaped leaves and clusters of apricot flowers in spring is at its best with the shrubby herbs, likewise the hybrid Juliana with its olive green foliage and clusters of lemon-yellow flowers in early summer. Like those of rosemary, the flowers are much visited by bees. These berberis grow 5–6 ft (1·5 m) tall.

Another attractive plant to accompany these herbs is *Ceanothus burkwoodii*, one of the Californian lilacs which has small dark green leaves which are evergreen and throughout summer it bears clusters of fluffy powder blue flowers. It is an excellent plant for a sunny wall where it will reach a height of 10 ft (3 m) and could be planted near rosemary which is always at its best on a wall. 'As for rosemary,' wrote Sir Thomas More, 'I let it run all over my walls, not only because the bees love it but it is the herb of love and remembrance'. Plants of old English lavender growing at the foot of an old brick or stone wall also lend a certain charm to a court-yard or walled garden and retain their leaves all winter.

Herbs for the shrub border

BAY (*Laurus nobilis*)   The Romans named it from the Latin, *laudis* (praise) and crowned their poets and victorious warriors with garlands made with its leaves. But it had a more practical use and warriors returning from battle or from a long march would place the leaves in their warm spring water baths to comfort their aching limbs as we could do today. Bay leaves and their twigs, burnt on an open fire, release a delicious perfume and they will add distinc-tion to *pot pourris* and sweet bags. The leaves also have culinary uses and are an important part of a *bouquet garni* used for roastings and stuffings. A single leaf included in marinades and preserves will give it an aromatic flavour and will add interest to a rice pudding and a glass of cold milk.

Native of southern Europe, the bay laurel is an evergreen shrub or small tree with lance-shaped leaves and in May and June bears inconspicuous yellow flowers followed by an ovoid fleshy berry. The plant will usually survive winter in the milder parts of Britain if sheltered from cold winds but it is best grown in a small tub so that it can be lifted indoors or into a greenhouse or shed about

1 December each year where it will remain until 1 April. If this is not practical, cover the heads with sacking during the same period. Bays are ideal plants to grow in a container, especially where grown as standards with a stem about 3–4 ft (1 m) long and the heads carefully clipped to form a circular or square head. Or they may be grown as a pyramid and are suitable to place on either side of a garden gate or door or to the entrance of the home. If protected in winter they will stay evergreen all year. In colder parts, the plants will lose their leaves but unless they are harmed by unduly severe weather, will come again in spring.

Bays are slow growing and require little pruning, no more than a gentle clipping in spring to maintain the shape. If growing in a tub, provide ample drainage and a compost made up of fibrous turf loam into which has been incorporated a small quantity of sand and a little decayed manure. Also give each tub 1 lb (450 g) of lime rubble or crushed chalk, worked well into the compost. Keep the compost comfortably moist during dry weather and give the plants a top dressing every spring.

Bays are propagated from cuttings of the new season's wood, removed in July, preferably with a 'heel' attached. Insert into pots filled with sandy compost after dipping the base of the cuttings in hormone powder to encourage quicker rooting.

COTTON LAVENDER (*Santolina incana*)   Due to its highly pungent foliage, it was considered to be the best of all moth deterrents and was dried and placed among church vestments, bed linen and also in clothes cupboards. The French call it *garde-robe* and it is a plant of the Composite order, in no way related to the ordinary lavender which is a labiate. Native of southern France, it may have come with the Normans or later. Parkinson (1629) wrote that it was found only in 'the gardens of great persons ... which doth cause it to be held in greater regard'. A perennial growing 2–3 ft (60–90 cm) tall and bushy, it can be clipped to any height from 12 in (30 cm) upwards and so is a useful edging plant. It is perennial, evergreen, and extremely hardy and is a valuable wind break for the most exposed gardens. The small linear leaves are like tiny lambs' tails and are silver-grey. The flowers are yellow and are borne in rounded heads in July and August. They are

39

most colourful but have the appalling smell of putrid meat which attracts flies for their pollination.

The plant has no culinary uses but an infusion of the leaves (a handful to 1 pt (570 ml) of boiling water) and taken when cold with a little lemon juice, will cleanse the kidneys and help in cases of jaundice.

Propagation is from cuttings removed with a 'heel' and inserted in sandy compost. Grow on in small pots when rooted.

CURRY PLANT (*Helichrysum angustifolium*)   A shrubby perennial, which in most parts of Britain is only half-hardy being native of South Africa; but unless killed during a severe winter, it will grow again in spring. It is a delightful acquisition for a shrub border with its bright silver foliage and it makes a low spreading bush 2 ft (60 cm) tall. The leaves have a hot curry-like taste and smell which they impart to soups and stews if used fresh after finely chopping, or when dried in winter. A little of the finely chopped leaves can be included in stuffings and in sausage meats but use sparingly as the flavour is pronounced.

Plant 20 in (50 cm) apart in a well drained sandy soil and a sunny position. To protect from winter frosts and cold winds, heap ashes over the roots and around the base of each plant and set other plants nearby which retain their winter foliage, to give protection.

Propagate by cuttings taken in late summer and inserted in sandy compost. When rooted, move to small pots and grow on under glass during winter and plant out in April. In this way, even if some plants are killed during winter, there will be others available to take their place.

GERMANDER (*Teucrium chamaedrys*)   Usually known as wall germander, for it is found growing on the old walls of castles and abbeys and is a low growing shrubby plant with dark green ovate leaves, hairy on the underside and bearing large rosy-purple flowers in a one-sided raceme. In Tudor times it was used to make 'knot' gardens for it can be clipped to make a low hedge and retains its foliage during winter but only in the south and west country. The leaves have a refreshing, lemon scent when pressed and, dried, are used in *pot pourris* and sweet bags. It was also one of Tusser's stewing herbs for, when trodden on, the leaves release their sharp, lemon scent. A decoction of the leaves, a small handful to ½ pt (275 ml) of boiling water and sweetened with a little honey, will ease a hard cough and clear the kidneys of impurities.

The plant grows 12 in (30 cm) tall and requires a well drained soil and sunny situation. It grows better if sheltered from cold winds. Propagation is by cuttings removed in July. Grow on under glass during winter and plant out in April.

LADIES' MAID (*Artemisia chamaemelifolia*)   It is a smaller edition of southernwood, growing rather less than 2 ft (60 cm) tall with finely divided leaves, like old lace, which emit a refreshing, fruity scent when handled. The plant is quite hardy but will usually lose its grey-green leaves in winter. When dry, they may be included in *pot pourris* and sweet bags to place among clothes as they are moth repellent. Propagation is from cuttings as for southernwood.

LAVENDER (*Lavendula spica*)   A shrubby perennial, native of southern Europe, and completely hardy in the British Isles. It has silver-grey foliage which is retained through winter and bears spikes of purple, blue or white flowers at the end of long erect stems. The plant takes its name from the Latin *lavare* (to wash) and, in Elizabethan times, a laundress was known as a 'lavendre', for it was usual to wash clothes in lavender water. It was the favourite scent of Queen Henrietta Maria, wife of Charles I and in her garden at Wimbledon a border of 'Rosemary, rue and white lavender' was grown.

Lavender requires a well drained calcareous soil and plenty of sunshine for it to produce plenty of essential oil. In the seventeenth century, it was realised that the south of England and East Anglia produced the world's finest lavender and commercial plantings were made in Surrey and Norfolk. The essential oil is contained in the tiny green bracts enclosing the flowers and to make the finest ottos the stems are excluded. From half a hundredweight of flower spikes, about 1 lb (450 g) of essential oil is obtained, the plants being at their best in their fifth or sixth years after which they are taken up and burnt, the smoke scenting the air for miles around on a calm day.

One part oil of lavender with three parts spirits of wine make an effective embrocation for sprains and three or four drops in a wineglassful of water will relieve palpitations and giddiness. It is also a valuable hair tonic when massaged into the scalp. A 'tea' made from the flowers and lemon rind, infused in hot water, will, if taken cold in hot weather, act as a restorative and is cooling.

The flowers are included in all *pot pourris* and sweet bags to place among clothes and a few flowers scattered into a salad will impart a pleasant balsamic flavour.

Where growing in a well drained calcareous soil, lavender will often seed itself and it transplants readily. It is also propagated from cuttings or pull-offs removed with a 'heel' in July and inserted in sandy compost. Plant the more robust old English lavender, *L. spica* at least 3–4 ft (1 m) apart if growing as a hedge and those of more compact habit, about 2 ft (60 cm) apart. Plant in spring and harvest the flowers in late summer when at, or just past, their best and during a period of dry weather. Cut the stems low down and place on trays in an airy room to complete the drying. Then rub the flowers from the stems into large bowls or boxes but retain the stems which will burn slowly like incense, after immersing in salt petre solution and drying. They will fill the home with their fragrance.

A lavender hedge may be kept in shape by judicious clipping. This should be done before it forms a mass of woody stems when clipping should not be attempted. There are numerous species and varieties. *L. spica* is that mostly grown commercially and its variety Seal not only contains more essential oil than all others but a five year plant will bear up to 1000 spikes. Grappenhall is the most vigorous and grows almost 4 ft (more than 1 m) tall and across while its flowers are of richest purple-blue with a powerful scent. *L. nana compacta* grows only half as high and makes a delightful hedge to surround a rose garden. The variety Hidcote bears purple-blue flowers and Alba, flowers of snow-white which are powerfully scented but the plant is less hardy than others. Twickle Purple is the darkest purple of all. The lavenders are much visited by bees and butterflies.

MARJORAM (*Origanum vulgare*) There are three forms; this, the Common or wild marjoram, present on hilly pastures and dry banks

Pot Marjoram

throughout England and Wales, and especially in Kent and Sussex, is a perennial plant growing 12 in (30 cm) tall, with small ovate leaves and bearing reddish-purple flowers in large cymes. *O. onites* is the pot marjoram, native of southern Europe, also perennial; and *O. marjorana*, the Sweet marjoram, used in *pot pourris* and scent bags which is perennial but because of its tenderness is often treated as an annual in the British Isles except in the south west.

The plant takes its botanical name from the Greek, *orosganos* (joy of the mountain) for when growing wild it is always a joy to behold, especially when in bloom; the scent of its leaves is sweet and aromatic. It figured in Isaac Walton's instructions for dressing a pike and the dried leaves are used in stuffings and to sprinkle on to soups and stews. It makes a most suitable seasoning for sausages and sausage meat and its flowering tops impart an aromatic flavour to home-brewed beers.

It is also used medicinally, a handful of tops placed in a warm bath will relieve nervous tension and a 'tea' made by infusing a handful of tops in 1 pt (570 ml) of boiling water will ease a nervous headache and if taken at bedtime will promote sound sleep.

O. onites, the Pot marjoram, is more pungent and can be used for everything the wild marjoram is used for and performs even better. This is the best one to grow in the garden and there is a handsome gold-leaf variety, *aureum*, which adds colour to the front of a border. Sweet marjoram is more sweetly scented than the others and, as Parkinson said, it was 'in demand by the ladies to put in nosegays' and to use 'in sweet powders, sweet bags and sweet washing waters'. In Stuart times, nosegays were carried about by the ladies to mask the unpleasant smells of the insanitary streets and this marjoram emits a delicious balsamic scent. From the cut stems it secretes an essential oil which smells of balsam. It was also known as Knotted marjoram for the flower buds first appear as tiny pale brown knots of string. This marjoram grows readily from seed, but the others do not and are propagated by cuttings of the half-ripened wood removed in July and inserted in a sandy compost. Plant out in spring, perhaps as an edging to the shrub border, planting 8 in (20 cm) apart or in small groups. The marjorams are as useful as the thymes and should be liberally planted.

Sweet marjoram is best grown as a half-hardy annual, the seed being sown in gentle heat in early March, in a greenhouse or frame or in a sunny window. Sow in pots or boxes of sandy compost and move to small pots when the seedlings are large enough to handle. Plant out in May, after hardening, and use the leaves and tops during summer. In autumn, cut the plants hard back and string up in bunches in an airy room to dry. Then rub down the leaves and use during winter. If the winter is mild or if growing in a west country garden, the plants may survive and come again in spring but seeds should be grown each year in case they do not.

MUGWORT (*Artemisia vulgaris*)   A shrubby perennial which grows 3–4 ft (1 m) tall, it has erect angled stems and dark green one or two pinnate leaves, covered with silvery down on the underside. The flowers, which are like those of mimosa, are borne in panicles from July to September.

The plant takes its name from the Saxon *moughte* (a moth) for it is moth repellent and a small sprig carried in the button hole will keep flies away in warm weather. The leaves were used to add their bitterness to ale before the introduction of hops. A nourishing drink is made by simmering 2 oz of the dried leaves with a gallon of water (or approx 50 gm in 4 litres) for an hour. Then add ½ lb (or 225 g) of brown sugar and, when dissolved, strain into an earthenware pan. Add a large teaspoonful of yeast and allow to ferment for ten to twelve days. When fermentation has finished, strain into bottles and cork tightly. It should be kept for a month or so in a dark place before it is used. Containing the bitter principle absinthin, it is a tonic and an appetiser. Take a wineglassful daily an hour before lunch.

Poultry keepers used to place the freshly chopped leaves in 'mash' to feed to chickens and turkeys for there is nothing like mugwort to keep them free from the usual poultry ailments. Countrymen would make a broth from the leaves and roots which was taken for gout and rheumatism. To ease sprains, they would make a warm concoction of the leaves, with those of agrimony and chamomile and apply it with a cloth to the painful part. With their bitterness, mugwort leaves are included in stuffings for the richer meats such as port and veal and to use with ducks and geese, to counteract their greasiness.

Plant at the back of the border, 3 ft (90 cm) apart and propagate from cuttings removed in July and rooted in a sandy compost, or from seed sown in pots or boxes in spring. Transplant to small pots when large enough and plant out the following April.

RED ROSE (*Rosa gallica* var. *officinalis*) A shrubby perennial of erect habit and growing 2 ft (60 cm) tall, it is included among the herbs for, since early history, it has been used for many of man's basic needs. It is probably the oldest garden plant known to us and was used to adorn the shields of Persian warriors 2000 BC. Native of the Near East, the plant may have been intro- duced into Britain by the Romans from occupied Gaul, hence its botanical name, and in the Middle Ages it became known as the Apothecary's rose for the dried petals were sold by apothecaries in winter not only to include in *pot pourris* and sweet bags to place among clothes (for this rose when dry, retains its perfume longer than all others) but because it had so many medicinal uses. Red Rose water, made by infusing a handful of fresh or dried petals in $\frac{1}{2}$ pt (275 ml) of boiling water and taken hot, will bring relief to those suffering from asthma. An ancient remedy for lung diseases was to pound red roses with a little sugar or honey, in a mortar and to take a teaspoonful twice daily. Red Rose water is astringent. Applied to the face it will tighten the skin and remove wrinkles, and binds in cases of dysentery and diarrhoea when taken internally.

The plant has persisted because, like most of the shrubby herbs, it flourishes in poor sandy soil but it will form new wood only if given a top dressing of decayed manure each autumn. It requires little pruning, apart from the removal of dead wood each year. Plant 2 ft (60 cm) apart, any time from November until March when the soil is in suitable condition.

ROMAN WORMWOOD (*Artemisia pontica*) Native of southern Europe, chiefly Italy, it grows about 3 ft (90 cm) tall and has finely cut leaves like those of southernwood but silvery-grey due to their being covered in hairs and without the refreshing, lemon scent of southernwood. It has the same bitterness as the common wormwood and is used to make Italian Vermouth 'to restore the mind', together with other herbs. An infusion of the tops in summer, a handful to 1 pt (570 ml) of hot water and sweetened with a little honey, is good for liver complaints and aids the digestion, especially if a small quantity if taken after a rich meal. It also makes an excellent tonic drink, a wineglassful being taken an hour before a meal. From the juice of fresh Roman wormwood, a tonic wine is made in Germany and which is taken just before a heavy meal to avoid sickness or digestive upset. Propagation is the same as for the common wormwood and it enjoys similar growing conditions, a well drained soil and an open situation.

ROSEMARY (*Rosmarinus officinalis*) A shrubby perennial of great hardiness although native of southern Europe and Mediterranean islands and taking its name from *ros-marinus* (dew of the sea). Retaining its foliage through winter, it comes into bloom early in spring when its porcelain blue flowers are frequented by bees. Its stalkless linear leaves have their oil ducts just below the surface and release their aromatic resinous scent in the slightest breeze or when one's clothes come into contact with the plant. For this reason, when there was no dry cleaning, rosemary bushes were planted on each side of a doorway so that the clothes of all who passed through would take on the same resinous perfume.

Growing up to 6–7 ft (2 m) high, rosemary is planted at the back of a shrub border where it will eventually grow as wide as it grows tall and will often survive for one hundred years or more with stems as thick as a man's arm. But it is at its best where growing against a sunny wall and can be tied in as it grows. It is also suitable to plant against a trellis, possibly at the back of the shrub border or where used to divide the herb garden from the rest of the garden. One of the most useful of all herbs, it was believed able to 'gladden the spirits', and 'refresh the mind' for no herb has a more up-lifting smell. An evergreen, the plant was used at funerals (to 'keep the memory green') and also at weddings. It was Shakespeare's 'herb of remembrance' and from it, Eau-de-Cologne is made which Napoleon used in large quantities to splash over his neck and shoulders after washing, to refresh himself on the battlefield.

A handful of the leaves or tops simmered for ten minutes in 1 pt (570 ml) of water and massaged into the scalp will promote the growth of new hair. Spirit of rosemary, kept by most stores, is used in the same way. An infusion of the tops added to a warm bath will ease tired limbs. Rosemary wine, made by pouring a half bottle of white wine on to a large handful of tops and allowing it to stand for a week before straining, can be taken, at bedtime as a carminative.

It has culinary uses, too, the flowers being included in an early summer salad and a sprig or two stuck into meat before roasting or grilling will impart a resinous scent and counteract the richness.

Rosemary requires a sandy calcareous soil and is propagated from cuttings, removed with a 'heel' and inserted in sandy compost; or from seed sown in a frame or in boxes in spring and planted out when large enough to handle.

RUE (*Ruta graveolens*)   Its leaf formation and blue-green colour combine to make it one of the most beautiful plants of the garden and Jackman's Blue, with its larger leaves of metallic blue, is an even more arresting sight. A perennial, rue is native of southern Europe but is completely hardy in the British Isles, coming through the severe winter of 1978-79 unscathed even near the east coast. It grows 2 ft (60 cm) tall and bears greenish-yellow flowers all summer. The plant takes its name from the Greek *reuo* (to set free) for it was used by the ancients to rid themselves of many

47

ailments. It is the most bitter herb and because of this has always been known as the Herb of Repentance or Herb of Grace. Parkinson said that 'it is a most wholesome herb' and because fleas kept well away from it, the leaves were placed on the bench of the dock at Assize Court whenever there was an outbreak of fever (carried by fleas) in Newgate Gaol. This symbolic gesture has continued from 1750 until today.

If the fresh leaves (and the plant retains its leaves all year) are placed on the buttocks and covered with a hot wet cloth or towel, they will relieve the pain of sciatica and ease rheumatic joints. An infusion of the leaves may be taken for epilepsy brought on by nervous strain. It acts as a tonic, too, being rich in mineral salts and will relieve indigestion. It has few culinary uses as it is too bitter but a sprinkling of finely chopped leaves in a cream cheese sandwich for example will add interest, or perhaps sprinkled over a salad.

Rue grows well in a calcareous soil but needs a well drained soil and a sunny situation. It is propagated from cuttings or grows readily from seed sown in pots or boxes in spring. Move the seedlings to small pots when large enough to handle and grow on until ready to plant out the following spring.

SAGE (*Salvia officinalis*)   A hardy evergreen shrubby herb growing about 20 in (50 cm) tall with square stems and wrinkled grey-green leaves and purple flowers borne from the axils of the leaves from July to September. The ancients believed the plant would give long life to all who used it hence its name *salvia* (salvation). Gerard said, 'it quickeneth the senses; strengtheneth the sinews; and restoreth health to those who have the palsy'.

To make a tonic drink, an infusion of a few leaves (fresh or dry) together with the rind of a lemon in 1 pt (570 ml) of boiling water and taken when cold, a wineglassful at a time, will enrich and purify the blood, restore after fatigue and help the digestion. If the tops are used, including the flowers, the drink will have a pleasant balsamic taste.

Sage cordial, made by boiling the leaves with the juice and rind of a lemon and a little honey will ease a cough. It is more effective if made from the red leaf sage.

For stuffings, and more sage is used than any other herb, it should be accompanied by a sprinkling of thyme and of pot marjoram. In Europe, sage has been used to flavour cheese since the days of Charlemagne and a few fresh leaves finely chopped, will add their particular savour to cheese sandwiches. The pineapple-scented sage, *Salvia nutilans*, one of the most delicious of all herbs, can be used fresh in a salad, together with slices of orange, to impart a rich fruity flavour. The purple flowers of sage may also be included in a salad, like those of rosemary and lavender.

Leaves of the broad-leaf sage dipped in batter and fried and then sprinkled with lemon juice, were served at the end of a rich meal, especially after mediaeval banquents, to aid digestion.

Sage requires a well drained soil and an open, sunny situation but as it is shallow rooting, it responds to a yearly top dressing of decayed manure. It also likes a soil containing lime or mortar and never grows well in an acid soil. It is propagated from cuttings taken in July, preferably with a 'heel' and rooted in a sandy compost; or from seed sown in spring in pots or boxes, or in shallow drills, transplanting in July to 18 in (45 cm) apart.

There is greater use for dried rather than fresh sage and the stems can be cut in June and bunched to string up in an airy room to dry, and again in September. This will keep the plants free from dead wood.

There is a broad-leaf and a narrow-leaf variety of sage, also a red-stemmed variety, *purpurea*, and its variegated form with leaves of carmine, green and cream. The pineapple leaf sage is *S. nutilans* and may be used in *pot pourris* and sweet bags.

SOUTHERNWOOD (*Artemisia abrotanum*) A shrubby perennial growing 3 ft (90 cm) tall with pinnate, grey-green leaves which usually fall in winter. The plant is called southernwood to denote its natural habitat of southern Europe: Wormwood grows in colder places. It is also known as Lad's Love and was included in lovers' posies. The French know it as *citronelle* because of its rich lemon fragrance. The leaves are included in *pot pourris* and sweet bags to place among clothes as it is moth repellent. It is also sleep inducing and a water made by immersing a handful of the leaves with those of Rosemary in 1 pt (570 ml) of boiling water and applied to the head by means of a cloth, will stimulate the hair glands and prevent the hair falling. It was also used in healing salves and ointments.

Southernwood requires an open, sunny situation and a well drained soil. It is propagated from cuttings of the half-ripened wood removed in July, preferably with a 'heel' and inserted in sandy compost. Pot on when rooted and plant out in April.

THYME (*Thymus vulgaris*)   The Common thyme is distinct from the prostrate thymes used to make a fragrant lawn or to plant between paving stone, in that it grows upright and about 10 in (25 cm) tall. It is a shrubby perennial of considerable hardiness though it may lose its leaves during a severe winter. The small oblong leaves are held on wiry stems and are dark green, grey on the underside while the purple flowers are borne in conical clusters. The entire plant has a rich pungent scent. Native of rocky ground of southern Europe and of several Mediterranean islands, it may have reached Britain with the Romans. With sage and rosemary, the thymes came to have more uses than any other herb. 'We preserve them with all the care we can in our gardens,' wrote Parkinson, 'for the sweet and pleasant scents they yield'. With rosemary or chamomile, an infusion made from the leaves and rubbed into the scalp will keep the head free of dandruff and the dried leaves put into muslin bags and placed among clothes will protect them from moths. The dried leaves too, are sprinkled over soups and stews and are made into stuffings to accompany pork and veal.

Common thyme requires a well drained soil and an open situation. Propagation is from cuttings removed with a 'heel' and rooted in sandy compost. When rooted, move to small pots from which the plants are set out in spring. Of all herbs, the thymes more than any resent root disturbance and should always be pot grown. They grow readily from seed sown in spring in pots or boxes and here too, as soon as large enough to handle they should be moved to small pots and planted out the following spring with the soil ball intact.

There are several interesting varieties of the common thyme, including Silver Posie which has purple stems and leaves splashed with silver; and *aureum* which has leaves splashed with gold.

WORMWOOD (*Artemisia absinthium*) A handsome perennial grow-ing 3 ft (90 cm) tall with twice-pinnate leaves which have blunt segments and are densely covered in down which gives them a greyish appearance. Tusser was scientifically correct when he recommended it as a tonic or restorative as the plant contains nitrate of potash. There is no better tonic than wormwood 'tea' made from an infusion of a handful of fresh or dried leaves in 1 pt (570 ml) of boiling water and taken, a wineglassful daily, sweetened with a little honey. The same infusion used hot on sprains and rheumatic joints will bring relief.

In mediaeval times it was one of the few plants known to counter-act the effects of poisonous plants and fungi and for this reason was held in great esteem while it was able to expel worms from the body. Today it is used in the manufacture of the liqueurs Absinthe and Chartreuse.

Like all the artemisias, it is moth repellent and cottagers would hang up the fresh stems in summer to keep the rooms free from flies and as Gerard said, it cooled the air in hot weather. In mediaeval times it was strewn over earth floors to keep them free from fleas.

A common plant of waste ground in all parts of the British Isles, it retains its leaves through winter and so can be used fresh all the year or dried, to make a tonic drink, as with mugwort. It is propagated in the same way, from cuttings or seed. The leaves give off a bitter pungent smell when pressed; with rue, it is the bitterest of all herbs.

Herbs for the shrub border

Herb	Botanical name	Height	Use
Bay laurel	*Laurus nobilis*	6 ft (2 m)	Culinary, pot pourris
Cotton lavender	*Santolina incana*	2 ft (60 cm)	Moth deterrent
Curry Plant	*Helichrysum angustifolium*	2 ft (60 cm)	Culinary

Growing Herbs

Herb	Botanical name	Height	Use
Germander	Teucrium chamaedrys	12 in (30 cm)	Medicinal
Ladies' Maid	Artemisia chamaemelifolia	2 ft (60 cm)	Pot pourris
Lavender	Lavendula spica	3–4 ft (1 m)	Pot pourris; medicinal
Marjoram, Sweet	Origanum marjorana	12 in (30 cm)	Pot pourris
Marjoram, Wild	Origanum vulgare	12 in (30 cm)	Culinary; medicinal
Mugwort	Artemisia vulgaris	3–4 ft (1 m)	Culinary; moth deterrent
Red Rose	Rosa gallica var. officinalis	2 ft (60 cm)	Pot pourris; medicinal
Roman Wormwood	Artemisia pontica	3 ft (90 cm)	Tonic
Rosemary	Rosmarinus officinalis	6 ft (2 m)	Culinary; medicinal
Rue	Ruta graveolens	2 ft (30 cm)	Moth deterrent; medicinal
Sage	Salvia officinalis	20 in (50 cm)	Culinary; medicinal
Southernwood	Artemisia abrotanum	3 ft (90 cm)	Moth deterrent
Thyme	Thymus vulgaris	10 in (25 cm)	Culinary; medicinal
Wormwood	Artemisia absinthium	3 ft (90 cm)	Tonic

Balm   Angelica   Agrimony

Herbs in the Flower Border

A large number of our most useful herbs have a beauty when in flower and leaf which is the equal of any of the most popular plants of the herbaceous border but unlike those herbs of shrubby habit, most die back in autumn and will come again in spring. They are completely hardy and are fully perennial and are increased by root division in spring or autumn or from offsets. With certain plants these may be seen growing around the plants and are lifted with a trowel without lifting the entire root. This can be done at almost any time between March and November; the offsets are replanted in the border and kept moist at the roots in dry weather.

A border filled with herbs will be colourful from early summer until late autumn when the foliage will begin to die back. Towards the end of November it is cut away just above soil level and burnt, while the ground around the plants is dug over and perhaps enriched with some garden compost or decayed manure. Those annual herbs which may have been growing in the border will be removed at the same time and destroyed, for by then, the seeds will have been harvested, as will the foliage if it is to be dried for use during winter.

Planting the border

The herb border should be planted exactly like any other herbaceous border, setting the taller growing plants to the back where they may be protected by a row of interwoven fencing panels or wattle hurdles. At the centre of the border plant those herbs which grow 2–3 ft (60–90 cm) tall, with the most compact to the front. As with most herbs, a sunny situation will be necessary but these herbs require a moister soil than do those of a shrubby nature described in the previous chapter. But though the soil must be moisture-holding in summer (and that means incorporating plenty of garden compost, decayed leaves or peat, and perhaps some decayed manure or used hops when the soil is dug over), it must also be well drained if the herbs are to survive excess moisture in winter. For this reason, herbs usually grow better in a porous soil rather than in clay soil. If the soil is heavy, work in plenty of drainage materials before adding the humus and remember to give it a good dressing of lime for no herbs do well in an acid soil. Do no planting until the soil is free from frost and is in a friable condition and keep the plants watered until established.

One should give as much thought to planning the border as one would do with any herbaceous border, setting out the plants in groups of two, three or four, with those of sparse foliage near those which have more leafy stems. Many herbs have yellow flowers but there are some with blue or purple flowers and the two are a pleasing compliment to each other. Some have silver-grey foliage, others dark green, and some emerald green. They should be grouped about the border so that when in full growth in summer, the whole border will be one of contrasting colours while the plants will be in daily use. A number of annuals and biennials, such as borage with its flowers of clear sky blue, alkanet and clary which are also blue, and marigolds with their flowers of brilliant orange or gold and which have so many uses, will add interest and colour to the border and should be included with those of perennial habit.

It may be advisable to stake those tall growing herbs to prevent them from being blown over by strong winds, unless the border is sheltered. If blown over, the plants will be deprived of sunlight and the leaves will not make their full amount of essential oil and so will be lacking in scent and flavour. For the same reason do not set the plants too close together. Give each one room to develop and they will have grown quite large in two or three years.

Herbs to grow in the flower border

AGRIMONY (*Agrimonia eupatoria*)   The agrimonys are among the loveliest of our wild flowers and are equally attractive in the garden. This, the common agrimony grows 2 ft (60 cm) tall, with slender reddish stems and leaves divided into four, five or six leaflets. The small deep yellow flowers are borne in long slender spikes in July and August. It takes its name from the Greek meaning 'shining' for it was thought that bathing the eyes in agrimony water removed cataract and made the eyes bright again. The plant contains tannin and an infusion of the leaves used as a gargle will ease a sore throat. Agrimony 'tea' drunk hot or cold is an excellent tonic drink and for its ability to stop internal bleeding it was included in the London *Pharmocopaeia*. It is a blood cleanser and placed in a warm bath it will relieve rheumatic pains.

In Fragrant Agrimony (*A. odorata*) the scent is more resinous, due to the presence of Borneol acetate as in pine leaves. The flowers are larger than those of Common agrimony and of deeper yellow. Its leaves, when dried, are used in *pot pourris*, and with hops and woodruff are used to stuff pillows to bring about sound sleep.

Both species are found in hedgerows and on grassy banks, mostly in south western England and Wales, and rarely in calcareous soils. Both plants are readily grown from seed sown in April in shallow drills and moved to the border when the seedlings are large enough to handle.

ANGELICA (*Angelica archangelica*)   A perennial, it differs from the wild angelica in that the stem is smooth and free from purple shading. The garden angelica has a powerful musky scent, much more pronounced than in the wild species. It was called angelica because its many valuable properties were thought to be of heavenly origin. It grows 5–6 ft (1·5 m) tall and has leaves 2 ft (60 cm) across. It bears greenish-white flowers in August but those should be removed before they open as they take the strength of the plant and may cause it to die back after a few years.

Angelica is carminative, being sleep-inducing and calming the

55

nerves. An infusion is made from the crushed roots, stems or leaves (1 oz (28 g) to 1 pt (570 ml) of boiling water), sweetened with honey, and taken at bedtime. The same, taken hot, will ease a tight chest. The seed is used by the monks of La Grande Chartreuse to flavour their world famous liqueurs, and the stems can be candied, to make a pleasant sweetmeat and to decorate cakes.

In a well drained soil it is a perennial, but is often treated as a biennial, seed being sown in early August where the plants are to mature. Allow 3 ft (90 cm) between the plants and if not allowed to flower it will be fully perennial. If one plant only is allowed to flower, it will seed itself each year and this is an easy and inexpensive way of growing it.

BALM (*Melissa officinalis*)   A perennial of great hardiness, it is one of the most useful of all herbs and because of the large amount of honey the flowers secrete, it should grow in the garden of all bee keepers. The plant grows 2 ft (60 cm) tall with upright hairy stems and with ovate leaves, emerald green in colour and deeply wrinkled. When pressed they emit a powerful smell of lemons, hence it is usually known as Lemon Balm.

During Tudor times it grew in every ale-house garden for, before hops were used, its leaves were used to clarify ale and to impart its refreshing flavour. The juice from the stems and leaves was rubbed on to furniture, to impart its refreshing smell and it was much in demand to weave into chaplets to wear at banquets in summer, when the air is often oppressive. Balm was the chief ingredient of Carmelite water, made by the nuns of the Abbey of St Justin in the fourteenth century and which was used as a toilet water by the people of mediaeval Europe long before Eau-de-Cologne was made.

Balm 'tea', made by immersing a small handful of leaves or tops in 1 pt (570 ml) of boiling water, is a tonic and aids the digestion. Add a little lemon juice and a small teaspoonful of honey and drink cold from the refrigerator. The young leaves, when chopped, make a pleasant addition to a salad and will impart a lemon taste to summer drinks. With rosemary, bay and sweet marjoram, they are included in green *pot pourris*.

It is a most attractive plant when in leaf and grows upright and bushy. So allow 2 ft (60 cm) between each plant. It requires a moist soil. Propagation is by root division in autumn when it has died down or early spring before it begins to grow again.

BERGAMOT (*Monarda didyma*) A hardy perennial growing 2–3 ft (60–90 cm) tall, it is one of the loveliest of herbs with square, deeply grooved stems and hairy leaves with serrated edges. The flowers, which are borne in whorls, are scarlet, pink or white with pale green bracts. If the leaves are handled, they release the delicious scent of bergamot orange and since its introduction from northern America in the eighteenth century, it has been used in green *pot pourris*, and in Europe is employed in the making of Eau-de-Cologne.

The plant was found in swampy ground near Oswego Bay on Lake Ontario where it was used to make a refreshing 'tea'. In England this became known as 'Oswego tea'. It is a tonic and tranquilliser and is made in the same way as balm 'tea'.

The fresh leaves and stems added to a warm bath will release a refreshing orange-like scent and will relieve tired limbs.

Like balm, it requires a moisture-holding soil and is propagated by root division and by offsets. Like most northern American plants it grows well in heavy soils and no amount of moisture will kill it. The best variety is Cambridge Scarlet which has flowers of glowing scarlet; Croftway Pink is also lovely.

BISTORT (*Polygonum bistorta*) A perennial growing about 16 in (40 cm) tall with arrow-shaped leaves of blue-green and from June to August, bearing small pink flowers in a compact spike. It takes its name from the Latin *bis* (twice) and *torta* (twisted) because of its snake-like rootstock, hence its other name of Snakeweed. The root is red and when dried and powdered and taken in a little red wine, helped in cases of 'spitting of blood' wrote John Pechey (1694), while it was also considered a cure for jaundice. The juice of the leaves heals body sores and rubbed on to the gums, will bring relief to toothache. The leaves were once used in stuffings but rarely so today as there are better herbs for the purpose.

A pleasing border plant, the best variety is superbum with its handsome spikes of deep reddish-pink. Propagate by division or from seed sown in pots or boxes in spring, planting out 12 in

(30 cm) apart in late summer when large enough to handle.

BURNET (*Poterium sanguisorba*)   An erect perennial growing 12 in (30 cm) tall, it is the Salad Burnet, a plant of more slender habit than the common burnet of pastures which sheep so much enjoy but both plants have a mild cucumber smell, like that of borage and were put into wine and cider, 'to quicken the spirits and refresh and cheery the heart'.

According to Pliny, the plant takes its name from the Greek *poterion* (a drinking cup). The leaves of Salad burnet are pleasant in salads and when included in cream cheese sandwiches.

The plant is styptic and the juice from the stems rubbed on to open cuts will stem the flow of blood.

The leaves are comprised of four to twelve pairs of opposite leaflets, as Turner so well described in his *Herbal* as 'like the wings of little birds'. The tiny flowers are green and purple tinted and borne in a capitate cyme but where growing in the garden the plants should not be allowed to flower. The plant will continue to grow all winter and is propagated by root division in March or from seed sown in shallow drills in April. Plant 10 in (25 cm) apart at the front of the border.

CATMINT (*Nepeta cataria*)   A perennial, closely related to ground ivy and deadnettle, growing 2 ft (60 cm) tall with square stems and heart-shaped, toothed leaves covered with down. Cats find the plant much to their liking and roll about the foliage for hours in ecstasy. The pinkish-mauve flowers are borne in whorls from June until September and the whole plant has a greyish appearance. The leaves were used for stuffings and seasonings but today other herbs are preferred.

Catnip 'tea' as it is called, calms the nerves and encourages sleep. It will also cause perspiration and so reduce a fever but should be taken in small doses, two teaspoonfuls for children; two tablespoonfuls for adults. Its taste is improved if some lemon peel is included with the infusion and then sweetened with a little honey. The 'tea' is made by infusing a handful of tops in 1 pt (570 ml) of boiling water, together with the lemon peel, or add a few drops of lemon juice. Ground ivy has the same medicinal qualities and may be used as an alternative.

Catmint is readily propagated by division of the roots in autumn or spring or from seed sown in spring in shallow drills, transplanting to the border when large enough to handle. Plant 18 in (45 cm) apart and it does well in ordinary soil.

CLARY (*Salvia horminoides*)   See the chapter on annual and biennial herbs.

COSTMARY (*Chrysanthemum balsamita*)   A perennial growing to 3 ft (90 cm) tall with entire leaves of deepest green and in July and August bearing heads of deep yellow flowers. Though native of central Asia, it has been a garden plant since earliest times, though has never become naturalised. The plant is dedicated to St Mary Magdalene and for short called Costmary or Maudlin. The tops were tied into small bunches with lavender flowers, 'to lie upon beds' and to place among linen and clothes. The leaves have a penetrating balsamic scent and were once used to flavour ale and wine. One leaf added to claret cup or cider will give it a delicious flavour. From the leaves a 'tea' is made which clears the kidneys of impurities. Used sparingly, the leaves when finely chopped, add interest when sprinkled over soups and stews.

Propagation is by root division in spring or from seed sown under cloches or in boxes in a frame in spring, planting in the border when large enough to handle.

COWSLIP (*Primula veris*)   A perennial growing in meadows and by the side of open woodlands, it is now rare in England and Scotland but is widespread in Ireland. The obovate leaves are deeply channelled, down which every drop of moisture from rain or dew is able to reach the roots without undue loss by evaporation. The drooping flowers are borne on a 6 in (15 cm) stem in umbels of six to eight and are pale yellow with an orange spot at the base of each petal. They are scented like a cow's breath, hence their name which is from the Anglo-Saxon *cusloppe* of the same meaning. Cowslips were associated with good husbandry and Shakespeare makes mention of this. It was a plant as much loved by the poets as the primrose and the violet and was also called paigle, from the Latin *prata*, a meadow where the plants mostly grew.

Cowslip

Cowslip wine, with its narcotic properties was made by all countrywomen, to enjoy in winter while the 'tea', made from an infusion of a handful of flowers in 1 pt (570 ml) of hot water and with a few drops of lemon juice added, will calm the nerves and bring about deep sleep if taken at bedtime. The same, applied to the face with lint, will remove blemishes and improve the complexion. Before lettuce came to be accepted as the chief ingredient of a salad, young cowslip leaves were included in all early summer salads, together with the flowers. They have the same slight bitterness as watercress which may be included with them.

Cowslips are propagated by root division in autumn or spring and are readily raised from seed sown in spring. As the seed is small, sow it in boxes of sterilised soil or the John Innes compost obtainable from garden shops or nurserymen and only just cover the seed. Place the boxes in a frame or sunny window and keep the compost moist. By the end of May, the seedlings will be ready to transplant, either to boxes of compost or to outdoor beds, where they grow on until November when they are moved to the front of the border. Cowslips enjoy deep planting and a soil containing some humus. They also appreciate a yearly mulch. They bloom rather later than the primrose, in May and June.

ELECAMPANE (*Inula helenium*) A perennial growing 5 ft (1·5 m) tall with downy, wrinkled leaves 12 in (30 cm) long and bearing the largest flowers of all our natural plants, being of golden-yellow (like single yellow chrysanthemums) and measuring up to 4 in (10 cm) across. It is in bloom July and August. Only the thick tuberous root is scented, when freshly lifted, smelling like ripe bananas but which takes on a violet perfume as it dries and the drier it becomes, the more powerful is the violet scent. A small piece thrown on to a low fire will fill the room with a violet perfume and in Elizabethan times, this was one of the most important ways of fumigating a house. The roots were also made into flat cakes of candied root by slicing through the roots when as thick as a man's arm. They make a pleasant sweetmeat and are eaten to relieve bronchitis and asthmatical complaints. The root contains a camphor-like substance, helenin, which is a powerful antiseptic and is said to be capable of killing the bacillus of tuberculosis. A decoction of the root will sweeten the breath and act as a tonic.

In northern America Elecampane is grown commercially for its roots, to provide all these medicinal requirements. Plants are raised from seed sown in spring, setting out the plants 3–4 ft (1 m) apart in autumn at the back of the border. It grows well in ordinary soil.

FEVERFEW (*Chrysanthemum parthenium*) A perennial growing about 16 in (40 cm) tall with pale green pinnate leaves divided into lobed segments and bearing small flowers in terminal clusters. The ray florets are white, the disc florets yellow and it blooms all summer. The plant emits a pungent smell when handled but at one time the double flowered variety and the golden-leaf form aureum, were popular summer bedding plants to accompany geraniums and calceolarias.

The dried leaves are moth repellent for the essential oil contains camphor. The leaves rubbed on insect bites will give immediate relief while a decoction of the leaves (a small handful to 1 pt (570 ml) of hot water with a little lemon juice and sweetened with honey) will ease a cough and break up phlegm. At one time the leaves were used in stuffings, but tansy, marjoram and sage are better for this purpose. Plants are raised from seed sown in gentle heat in early March, the seedlings being grown on in small pots and planted out in early June.

61

FENNEL (*Foeniculum vulgare*)   An erect perennial growing 4–5 ft (about 1·5 m) tall, its three to six pinnate leaves divided into narrow segments and bearing yellow flowers in large umbels. They are followed by seeds which are blunt at each end. The seeds, leaves and stems have the pleasing smell of newly mown hay which is retained when the plant is dried. It may have been introduced by the Romans who made it into wreaths to wear as an emblem of flattery. The seed was used to flavour bread and cakes and later came to be used, as a substitute for juniper, to flavour gin.

Like dill, fennel is a carminative, and, to relax nervous tension, take a wineglassful of fennel water sweetened with honey, at bed-time. Fennel water also promotes the secretion of milk with nursing mothers, and used slightly warm to bathe the eyes, it removes inflammation.

Fennel also has many culinary uses. It makes a delicious sauce to serve with fish, especially mackerel and eel, which Henry VIII so much enjoyed. The leaves are included in soups and stews while the stems can be stewed until tender and served with meats.

The plant grows best in a well drained calcareous soil and is best propagated from seed which is sown in pots or boxes in spring, setting out the young plants towards the end of summer. Plant 3–4 ft (1 m) apart and if the seeds are to ripen, it needs a sunny situation.

HERB BENNET (*Geum urbanum*)   The Wood Avens is an erect hairy perennial growing 16 in (40 cm) tall with pinnate leaves and bear-ing small, golden-yellow flowers. It is widespread in woodlands but is not at all common. A pleasant plant for the herb garden or border, it has clove-scented roots. After cleaning and washing, a small piece may be included in wine or ale as an alternative to clove-scented pinks, and the root grated into an apple pie will act as a substitute for cloves. A ½ oz (14 g) of the dried and sliced root immersed in 1 pt (570 ml) of boiling water and sweetened with a little honey is inducive to sound sleep if a wineglassful is taken at bedtime, and taken hot it warms the stomach and expels wind. In earlier times, the dried roots were placed among bedding and vestments, to impart a clove-like scent and keep away moths.

Plant 10 in (25 cm) apart and propagate by root division in spring or from seed sown in shallow drills in April.

HYSSOP (*Hyssopus aristatus*)   An evergreen perennial growing 2 ft (60 cm) tall with elliptic leaves and bearing sage-like flowers in short racemes. The flowers are blue or pink and are much visited by bees and butterflies. Native of central Europe, it is hardy and withstands clipping so that it was used, with marjoram, savory and thyme, to make knot gardens 'for these endure all the winter through greene,' wrote Thomas Hyll. In *Othello*, Iago suggests that to 'set hyssop and weed up thyme' alluding to the manner in which one should act, might be advisable, thus showing the esteem the plant was held in. It was used for strewing and is an essential ingredient of *pot pourris* and sweet bags. The leaves were bound over wounds when they would bring about rapid healing. The poet Spenser wrote of 'sharpe isope' and the leaves will indeed impart a 'sharp' aromatic taste to soups and stews but must be used sparingly.

Grow it with those herbs of shrubby characteristics or in the flower border for it is a handsome plant and grows upright but bushy. Plant 2 ft (60 cm) apart and propagate by root division or from cuttings, while it comes readily from seed sown in shallow drills in spring. Known as the Holy Herb, it takes its name from the Hebrew *azob* (a Holy plant).

LADY'S SMOCK (*Cardamine pratensis*)   An unbranched perennial with flower stems growing 15 in (38 cm) tall from a rosette of dark green leaves. The flowers, which are borne in clusters from April to July are of an unusual shade of metallic mauve. It is a plant of damp meadows, common by the banks of the Avon and Dove and other rivers of the Midlands. It is a handsome plant for the flower border especially the double variety, *flore plena* and takes its name Cardamine from the belief that it strengthened the heart. Of the same *Cruceriferae* family of plants as the nasturtium and watercress, people of earlier times realised that its leaves were nourishing and kept away scurvy. This is now substantiated by scientific research for they contain iron and sulphur salts and are rich in vitamin C. The leaves were included in early salads and placed in farm workers' sandwiches, with cheese. They have the same pleasantly bitter taste as watercress.

The plant requires a damp moisture-holding soil and is tolerant of semi-shade. It is propagated by root division in autumn, replanting the offsets 12 in (30 cm) apart or from seed sown in spring in shallow drills. The plant is also able to reproduce itself from tiny plantlets which appear on the leaves. If the leaves are laid on the surface of a box of soil towards the end of summer and kept comfortably moist, the plantlets will have formed good sized plants to set out the following spring.

MALLOW (*Althaea officinalis*) A hoary perennial growing 3–4 ft (1 m) tall with three to five lobed leaves covered with short hairs which gives the plant a greyish appearance. The large cup-shaped flowers, borne in axillary cymes are of a lovely shade of soft mauve-pink. The flowers, which appear in August and September are followed by round seeds which have a pleasant nutty flavour which children like to chew. Though a handsome border plant, and in the wild to be found by the roadside everywhere, it seeds itself so readily and the roots are so large and penetrating that unwanted plants should be eradicated as seedlings wherever they appear.

The plant takes its name from *althos* (a remedy) and its name mallow is from *Malassein*, alluding to its demulcent qualities which are the equal of slippery elm. The roots contain half their weight of saccharine viscous mucilage so that they are soothing to the stomach taken internally and externally if fomentations are applied. To 1 oz (28 g) of the dried root, add 1 pt (570 ml) of water and boil for 10 minutes, then strain. Take for cases of diarrhoea and dysentery. The leaves, after boiling for a few minutes and placed in a muslin bag for applying to bodily aches and sprains, will give quick relief, likewise if placed in a warm bath. A pleasant summer drink is made from the leaves and flowers which is refreshing.

The mallow grows in ordinary soil and does well in the poorest of soils, coming readily from seed sown in shallow drills in spring. Move to the border when large enough to handle. Mature plants are difficult to divide as they form a large thick tap root.

MEADOWSWEET (*Filipendula ulmaria*) A perennial growing 3–4 ft (1 m) tall with wiry stems and pinnate leaves, dark green above, grey on the underside and releasing an aromatic scent when pressed. Ben Jonson called it Meadow's Queen for when in bloom, from June to September, the plant takes on a stately appearance with its crowded cymes of cream-coloured flowers. They have an unpleasant smell but the aromatic foliage contains oil of wintergreen and it was a favourite strewing plant. It takes its name from the Latin, *ulmus* (an elm tree) for its leaves are of similar appearance. It is present in damp woodlands and in low lying meadows throughout the British Isles, usually in limestone districts.

Parkinson said that a leaf placed in a glass of wine 'will give as quick and fine a relish thereto as Burnet will'. It has no culinary uses but the plant is astringent and the fresh or dried leaves (a large teaspoonful when dried) infused in 1 pt (570 ml) of hot water and sweetened with honey, will, if a wineglassful is taken twice daily, clear up diarrhoea and colic of the stomach and is safe for children. The same can be taken daily during summer, with ice, and is a refreshing tonic drink.

The plant requires a soil containing some humus and one which is not lacking in lime. Propagation is by root division in late autumn or by seed sown in shallow drills in spring, transplanting the young plants to the border early in autumn.

MULLEIN (*Verbascum thapsus*)   Though a biennial, this handsome plant is for the flower border where it will grow up to 6–7 ft (2 m) tall in a few months, its large lanceolate leaves being so densely covered in down as to feel thick and woolly to the touch, like cloth and give the plant a silver-grey appearance. The flowers are of a lovely biscuit colour and are borne in a dense terminal spike from June to August. The plant is widespread in southern England and East Anglia, usually on dry banks and on waste ground by the roadside, preferring a well drained, sandy soil.

It takes it name from the Latin *barbascum*, a beard, from the white hairs which cover all parts of the plant. The thick leaves were placed in children's shoes to give the feet protection when walking to school along the roughly surfaced roads, and cottagers would burn the thick stems which they made into tallow, hence the plant's name of candlewick.

It was in demand for the relief of pulmonary consumption. The leaves were boiled in milk for ten minutes and, after straining and sweetening with honey, a wineglassful was taken twice daily. A 'tea', made by an infusion of the flowers and leaves in hot water and sweetened with honey, is a sedative if taken at bedtime and is a useful cure for gout. The oil made by steeping the flowers in olive oil in the sunlight for about a month, was the countryman's standby for earache, just two or three drops being placed in the ear and is a reliable remedy for piles. The plant has no culinary uses.

It readily seeds itself, the old plants being removed late in autumn after shedding their seeds. It is not deep rooting while the young plants move easily. As many as possible should be allowed to grow on at the back of the border where it is so effective.

RAMPION (*Campanula rapunculus*)   See the chapter on annual and biennial herbs.

ROSE-ROOT (*Sedum roseum*)   A hardy perennial, it is of the Stonecrop family of succulents with fleshy leaves, pointed at the apex and grey-green in colour. They store water and are able to survive long periods of dry weather. Growing about 12 in (30 cm) tall, the greenish-yellow flowers have purple anthers and are borne in a terminal inflorescence. Found on cliffs and rocky slopes from North Yorkshire to the far North East of Scotland and in Wales and the Isle of Man, only the roots are scented, emitting the scent of red roses as they dry. From the roots, a distilled water is obtained, smelling of roses, which was at one time used to improve the complexion and to sprinkle on clothes.

The plant can be grown to the front of a border but is at its best on a low wall, planting it with the creeping thymes and other low-growing plants. It requires an open sunny position and a well drained soil. It is best propagated by offsets, removing pieces of the plant with some roots attached or from seed sown in spring in pots or boxes, setting out the plants in early autumn.

SOAPWORT (*Saponaria officinalis*)   A handsome glabrous perennial growing 2 ft (60 cm) tall with broad lanceolate leaves of brightest green and bearing pale pink flowers in large corymbs from July until October. It is usually found by ponds and streams, possibly as a garden escape and is more familiarly known as Bouncing Bet.

The plant used to be found in every cottage garden for, when soap was too expensive to buy, a lather could be obtained from soapwort, all parts of which contain the principle saponin. The leaves and stems were crushed and placed in a bowl of warm water when they would produce a considerable lather. The juice was also rubbed on to abrasions and would speed healing.

A plant of easy culture, it grows well in ordinary soil provided it contains some humus. The best form is the double flowered and there is a double white, *alba plena* which has contrasting dark foliage. They are propagated by root division but the single flowered is readily grown from seed sown in April.

ST JOHN'S WORT (*Hypericum perforatum*) The Common St John's Wort is a hardy evergreen perennial growing 2 ft (60 cm) tall and the same across. The small elliptic leaves are covered with pellucid dots or glands which when handled emit an unpleasant smell, like goats, but no plant has more medicinal properties. An infusion of the leaves, a small handful to a pint of boiling water, and sweetened with a little honey, will relieve a hard cough and if a wineglassful is taken an hour or so before bedtime, it will prevent children from wetting the bed. From the leaves and flowers, an ointment is made which quickly heals bed sores and burns if the skin is unbroken.

A common plant of sandy banks and deciduous woodlands of the Midlands and southern England, it grows well in ordinary soil and in semi-shade. Propagation is by root division or from cuttings taken in July, preferably with a 'heel' and rooted in sandy compost.

TANSY (*Tanacetum vulgare*) A perennial growing 3 ft (90 cm) tall with dark green fern-like leaves divided into several pairs of pinnatifid leaflets and tiny button-like flowers borne in flat heads. The essential oil stored in the leaves is released as a camphor-like smell when the leaves are handled. The leaves were shredded into eggs and beaten up and fried as flat cakes called 'tansies' to be eaten during Lent in remembrance of the bitter herbs of the Passover. A delicious herb butter is to be made by finely chopping a leaf or two of tansy, with sage and balm and adding them to $\frac{1}{2}$ lb (225 g) of butter. This is beaten to a creamy consistency and used as a spread for cheese or tomato sandwiches. The leaves are included in stuffings and may be sprinkled into soups and stews.

A soothing complexion milk is made by soaking a handful of leaves in buttermilk for ten days, then straining into bottles. Tansy 'tea', made by immersing a handful of leaves or tops in 1 pt (570 ml) of hot water and flavoured with a little lemon juice and honey, will act as a tonic and purify the blood. Take a wineglassful each day before lunch.

A handsome border plant, tansy has a creeping rootstock and is propagated by lifting the stems with some roots attached and replanting 18 in (45 cm) apart. Ordinary soil containing a little humus is suitable and an open situation. The fern-leaf form, *foliis crispis* is an effective plant for the front of a border for it has emerald green foliage and grows only 15 in (38 cm) tall.

TARRAGON (*Artemisia dracunculus*)   A perennial growing about 2 ft (60 cm) tall with lance-shaped leaves and drooping white flowers borne in flat heads. This form is known as French tarragon (to distinguish it from the Russian variety) and reached England during Tudor times. Parkinson said it was like 'a long-leaved hisop ... of a taste not unpleasant but which is somewhat austere with the sweetness'.

Tarragon vinegar, made by immersing the leaves in white wine vinegar, is the principle ingredient of sauce tartare and the French also use it in their famous Dijon mustards. To make the vinegar, fill a large earthenware jar with leaves which have had their stalks removed and fill up with white wine vinegar or best malt vinegar. Allow to stand for fourteen days, then strain into bottles and use as required for sauces and mustards. A mayonnaise is greatly improved by adding a little tarragon vinegar to it.

Like parsley, tarragon freezes well. After cutting the stems, blanch for a minute before placing in plastic bags and into the freezer. The leaves will retain their flavour if frozen in ice cubes. The leaves are also used in stuffings and are sprinkled over soups and stews after finely chopping, or use them when dried.

Tarragon is propagated by root division in autumn or from cuttings taken in July and rooted in a sandy compost. Cover with a plastic bag, when rooting will take place in about six weeks. Move to small pots and plant out in spring 18 in (45 cm) apart. It requires a well drained soil and an open situation.

VERVAIN (*Verbena officinalis*) A hairy perennial growing about 16 in (40 cm) tall, with square stems and toothed unstalked leaves. The flowers are pale mauve and appear from July until September. A common plant of wasteland and hedgerows, it is attractive in the border.

It has long been the plant most often used by witches to make their spells and it was held in great esteem by the Druids. But it has better uses. Pasteur recommended it as an excellent hair tonic if vervain water is massaged into the scalp and an infusion of the whole plant in boiling water and allowed to cool, will give a sparkle to the eyes if used daily as an eyewash. An infusion of the leaves and tops, sweetened with a little honey and taken warm last thing at night, encourages sound sleep for it is a carminative.

Vervain likes a well drained soil and is readily grown from seed sown in pots or boxes in spring, or in shallow drills, setting out the plants when large enough to handle.

WOOD BETONY (*Stachys betonica*) See the chapter on medicinal herbs and their uses.

YELLOW GENTIAN (*Gentiana lutea*) A handsome perennial growing 4–5 ft (1·5 m) tall with large oblong leaves and yellow flowers which appear in whorls from near the top of the stems during July and August. Native of deciduous woodlands of central Europe, it is found in similar places in England as a garden escape.

In Britain and in Europe, since earliest times, a tonic drink known as Gentian Bitters has been made from the roots which are black on the outside when lifted, and yellow inside. Like burdock it clears the blood and tones the system. Culpeper said that if the dried roots were steeped in white wine for several weeks 'it would refresh those that are weary with travel and grown lame in their joints'. The roots grow large and the plants should not be disturbed until several years old during which time the border will be enhanced by the beauty of the plants. Lift in late autumn and to maintain a supply, replant the smaller offsets. Alternatively, plants are readily raised from seed sown in spring in shallow drills. Ordinary soil is suitable and the plant is tolerant of semi-shade.

YELLOW LOOSESTRIFE (*Lysimachia vulgaris*) A perennial growing 3–4 ft (1 m) tall and increasing by its underground rootstock. The lance-shaped leaves are formed in whorls and covered by black dots, and the bright yellow flowers are borne in panicles from the axils of the upper leaves during July and August. It is found on moist ground, by ponds and streams. In early times the plant was tied up in bunches and hung from the ceiling of rooms in summer for it would keep away flies and for the same reason, travellers on foot would seek it by the wayside and pick a sprig or two to carry with them or sit down beside it to eat their lunch, untroubled by flies and midges. The plant contains tannin and the leaves and stems infused in boiling water and allowed to cool will ease a sore throat if used as a gargle. The juice has antiseptic powers and if rubbed on to cuts and abrasions, it quickly heals them.

Pieces of root with a stem are detached in autumn and replanted into a soil containing humus. Allow 2 ft (60 cm) between the plants as they will increase rapidly and soon grow into each other but it is a handsome plant for the middle of a border.

Herbs for the border and their uses

Herb	Botanical name	Height	Use
Agrimony Common	*Agrimonia eupatoria*	2 ft (60 cm)	For internal bleeding; tonic drink
Agrimony Fragrant	*Agrimonia odorata*	2 ft (60 cm)	In *pot pourris*; pillows
Angelica	*Angelica archangelica*	5–6 ft (1·5 m)	Carminative; flavouring
Balm	*Melissa officinalis*	2 ft (60 cm)	*Pot pourris*; tonic drink; salads
Bergamot	*Monarda didyma*	2 ft (60 cm)	Oswego 'tea'; *pot pourris*; baths
Bistort	*Polygonum bistorta*	16 in (40 cm)	Jaundice; to heal body sores
Burnet (Salad)	*Poterium sanguisorba*	12 in (30 cm)	In salads; in drinks

Herb	Botanical name	Height	Use
Catmint	*Nepeta cataria*	2 ft (60 cm)	Carminative; to reduce body temperature
Costmary	*Chrysanthemum balsamita*	3 ft (90 cm)	To cleanse the kidneys; to flavour drinks
Cowslip	*Primula veris*	6 in (15 cm)	In salads; to make wine; carminative
Elecampane	*Inula helenium*	5 ft (1·5 m)	Antiseptic; for asthma
Feverfew	*Chrysanthemum parthenium*	16 in (40 cm)	For coughs; moth repellent
Fennel	*Foeniculum vulgare*	4–5 ft (1·5 m)	Carminative; to flavour sauces and soups and stews
Herb Bennet	*Geum urbanum*	16 in (40 cm)	Sleep inducing; roots for flavouring
Hyssop	*Hyssopus aristatus*	2 ft (60 cm)	In *pot pourris*; to flavour soups and stews
Lady's Smock	*Cardamine pratensis*	15 in (38 cm)	In salads
Mallow	*Althaea officinalis*	3–4 ft (1 m)	Demulcent
Meadowsweet	*Filipendula ulmaria*	3–4 ft (1 m)	Astringent; to flavour drinks
Mullein	*Verbascum thapsus*	6–7 ft (2 m)	For earache; sleep inducive
Rose-root	*S. roseum*	12 in (30 cm)	Rose-scented water
Soapwort	*Saponaria officinalis*	2 ft (60 cm)	For washing
St John's Wort	*Hypericum perforatum*	2 ft (60 cm)	To relieve coughs; prevent bed wetting
Tansy	*Tanacetum vulgare*	3 ft (90 cm)	Tonic drinks; complexion aid
Tarragon	*Artemisia dracunculus*	2 ft (60 cm)	To make vinegar and sauces
Vervain	*Verbena officinalis*	16 in (40 cm)	Eye lotion; hair tonic
Yellow Gentian	*Gentiana lutea*	4–5 ft (1·5 m)	Tonic drink
Yellow Loosestrife	*Lysimachia vulgaris*	3–4 ft (1 m)	Sore throat; fly repellent

Thyme

Carpeting Herbs - To Make a Fragrant Path and Lawn

Among the most delightful of all herbs are those of prostrate habit. These form dense low clumps which spread out to cover large areas of soil suppressing annual weeds if planted near together, and forming in due course, a 'lawn' of a different type and of greater interest than one made of grass. The same plants may be used to set between crazy paving or flag stones which they will partly cover in a most attractive way. Indeed, if there is a part of the garden that can be paved or set with old bricks, this will be an attractive feature and will provide interest the whole year round, often when the rest of the garden is too wet to walk upon. A path made of bricks or stone paving, leading from one part of the garden to another will be a most useful asset for it will quickly dry after rain or snow and enable one to move from one part of the garden to another without needing to put on protective footwear or harming the wet ground by treading.

There are a number of plants which possess the necessary characteristics, the most important being that they do not resent being trodden upon, while those grown for their herbal qualities will release a refreshing pungent scent whenever their foliage is crushed under foot or, where used to make a 'lawn', sat on in summer. The lawns of Elizabethan gardens were not made of the high quality grass as they later came to be made. They were composed of plants of creeping, prostrate habit, such as chamomile, of which Falstaff said to Prince Henry, later to become King Henry V, 'Harry, I do not only marvel where thou spendest thy time, but also how thou art accompanied, for though the chamomile, the more it is trodden, the faster it grows, yet youth, the more it is wasted, the sooner it wears'. There are other plants of which the same may be said, especially the low-growing thymes and mints. It was Francis Bacon who wrote of 'those flowers which perfume the air most delightfully ... being trodden upon and crushed are Burnet, Wild Thyme and Water Mint; therefore you are to set whole alleys of them, to have the pleasure when you walk or tread'.

Preparing the ground

To make a fragrant 'lawn', which like grass remains green all year but which, unlike grass, will need cutting at the most twice yearly, well drained ground is necessary. Most of the carpeting plants require a light, sandy soil from which excess winter moisture can readily drain away. At the same time, the plants must be able to tolerate long periods of warm, dry weather and none is better able to do so than the herbs. If the soil is heavy, first apply a dressing of caustic (unhydrated) lime in autumn. This is obtainable from a builder's merchant and is incorporated into the soil as it is turned over. When moisture comes into contact with the lime, it causes a violent reaction which disintegrates the lime and with it the clay particles of the soil. Winter frosts and winds will complete the break up of the clay and by early April the lawn can be planted. A heavy soil may also be made more porous by incorporating some grit or shingle such as boiler ash or crushed brick, also clearings from ditches, and this will enable winter moisture to drain away more easily. If soil is sandy, peat is also valuable, having the opposite effect and enabling the soil to hold more moisture in summer. A light, sandy soil can be made more retentive of moisture if some humus is added when the ground is prepared and this is done just before planting. Work in material from the compost heap or used hops, obtainable from a brewery usually for the asking, or decayed leaves. Such a soil is easily worked and presents few problems.

Where there is little depth of soil, this can be increased by 'green' manuring. In early spring, thickly scatter rape seed over the surface and rake it in. Keep it watered and within a month it will have grown several inches (centimetres) tall and will also have formed a thick mat of fibrous roots below the surface. The plants can then be dug in and will increase the depth of top soil and humus content.

The soil of a town garden, which may have become too acid to grow herbs, will benefit from a liberal dressing of hydrated lime applied to the surface in winter. Give 1 oz/yd² (35 g/m²) and rake it in. During winter, when the frost is out of the ground, turn over the surface and leave it rough until spring by which time the frosts will have broken the soil down so that before planting, it can be brought to a fine tilth.

Herbs will grow well in poor soil so long as it is not too acid, and a bank exposed to the sun, can be planted with the low-growing carpeting plants, especially the wild thymes which are found growing on mountainous slopes. 'I know a bank where the wild thyme grows' wrote Shakespeare and the plants are to be found on well drained slopes. To keep the plants in shape, clip them with shears occasionally and they require no other attention.

A fragrant 'lawn' can be made anywhere in an open, sunny position, away from overhanging trees. It could be made to any width and to any length and will look most attractive if made along one side of a path, possibly with a border of herbs on the other side, backed by interwoven fencing as protection from cold winds. If the path can be made of York stone or of old red bricks, placed on their sides, the same plants used for the 'lawn' can also be used to decorate the path.

To make a path

To make a path, begin by marking out the necessary width and length. Then remove soil to the depth of the paving stone or the bricks which are placed on their side. It may be thought advisable to give the path a concrete bed over which the stones (or bricks) are set to prevent weeds appearing between the stones, but laying the stones on 2 in (5 cm) of compacted sand will have much the same effect and will be more easily done. An even better job can be done if a base of similar depth is made of crushed brick or clinker and over this a layer of sand is placed, making the surface level and as firm as possible. If 2 in (5 cm) is allowed for the depth of the stones or bricks, then it will be necessary to remove soil to a depth of 6 in (15 cm) so that the top of the path is level with the surrounding ground. Even if using paving stones rather than bricks, a straight edge of bricks placed on their sides, will provide the path with a neat finish and enable the stones to be laid more easily.

To make the path the only tools required are a spade and builder's spirit level. If two edges of bricks are laid, working to two garden lines which show the correct width and length of the path, it is a simple matter to set the bricks and then the stones to the correct height and level by using the spirit level placed across the path. If using York paving stones, first sort out the pieces and place in their various sizes and make sure you have the flattest surface to the top so that it will present little discomfort when walking over the path or difficulty when wheeling a barrow over it. It will be necessary to place the straightest edge to the sides, whether brick edges are used or not.

Before the first stones are laid, make sure that the sand or concrete base is as level as possible, then begin laying the stones at one end and work along the entire length of the path, placing the stones as close together as possible to prevent weeds appearing between them. Small pockets can be left here and there, at intervals of about 2 ft (60 cm) and these will be filled with soil or will accommodate the soil ball of the plant if it is pot grown. A pot grown plant will quickly establish itself and may be planted at any time except when the weather is severe.

A fragrant lawn

Where planting a herb 'lawn', and chamomile will be the most important of all the herbs on account of its low, spreading habit, set out the plants about 6 in (15 cm) apart and during the first summer, keep the plants well watered. The 'lawn' will have rather a sparse appearance for twelve months and no cutting is done the first year. If any plants die, fill in the gaps with seedlings specially grown for the purpose and by the second summer begin to roll the 'lawn', exactly as for a grass lawn. In August, take the shears gently over the plants to remove any flower heads or long shoots. Early in autumn it may be possible to cut the 'lawn' with a mower if the blades are raised as high as they will go. Treading the plants will also keep them short and encourage them to spread and, if the ground is well drained, it will be possible to walk over the plants at almost any time, except perhaps during the mid-winter months. If the creeping thymes are used with or without chamomile, they will provide a blaze of vivid colour all summer and the 'lawn' will release a refreshing scent when walked upon. What is more, those herbs used to decorate a path or to make a 'lawn' will provide the household with leaves and flowers for many purposes, for a hair rinse and to include in smoking mixtures, for *pot pourris* and to use in the kitchen. Such a 'lawn' will not only be labour-saving when established, but useful too, and the plants will remain green through winter.

Until the plants begin to spread out and suppress annual weeds, it will be necessary to weed between them during their first year but disturb them as little as possible. Perennial weeds will have been removed before any planting was done.

If the creeping thymes and other low growing herbs are to be used with chamomile, plant the chamomile 10 in (25 cm) apart each way and at the centre of the square, put in a creeping thyme.

Herbs to use for a 'lawn' or path

CALAMINT (*Calamintha ascendens*) Named after the Greek *kalos* (beautiful) and *minthe* (mint) from the beauty of the plant and its mint-like smell which it releases when the leaves are pressed or the plant is trodden upon. From it an aromatic 'tea' is made which warms the stomach and relieves indigestion. It is a carminative and used in cases of hysteria.

It is a low-growing perennial with a creeping rootstock and square stems covered in short downy hairs. The leaves are serrated at the edges while the lilac-pink flowers are borne in forked axillary cymes. A labiate, more like a thyme than a mint, the lower lip of the corolla is lobed and covered in tiny purple spots. In bloom from July to September, it is also known as Basil thyme and is present on dry banks, in calcareous soil in England and Wales and on the west of Ireland but is rare in Scotland. It can be planted between paving stones or as an edging to small beds of herbs for it is of shrubby habit and retains its foliage all winter except in the severest weather.

It is propagated from cuttings, taken in July and rooted in pots of sandy soil. Move to small pots when rooted and plant out in April. Plants may also be raised from seed sown in pots or boxes in spring. Move to small pots when large enough to handle and plant out the following spring.

Camomile

CHAMOMILE (*Anthemis nobilis*)   The low-growing common chamomile as distinct from *A. tinctoria*, is a border perennial which grows 2 ft (60 cm) tall, with a much-branched stem and leaves cut into segments. The long-stalked flowers droop before they open and have white ray-florets and yellow disc-florets and appear from June to August. All parts of the plant are useful. The plant derives its name from the Greek meaning 'earth apple', from the refreshing apple scent of the plant when handled or trodden upon. In Spain it is called manzinella, little apple, and because of its almost prostrate form, the plant has always been the symbol of humility.

To make a chamomile 'lawn', seed is sown in drills made 6 in (15 cm) apart. Sow thinly so that there is no over-crowding and when large enough to handle, set out the plants where the 'lawn' is to be made. They readily transplant. A 1 oz (28 g) packet of seed will produce about 1000 plants, enough to make a large 'lawn' though some should be kept in reserve, to fill in if any plants die back. As chamomile is hardy and quick growing, and inexpensive, whether grown from seed or plants are obtained from specialist growers, it should form the best part of the 'lawn' and indeed, a 'lawn' made entirely of chamomile will be one of beauty at all times of the year, of brightest emerald green and it will have a long life. It also has many uses.

The dried and ground leaves are the main ingredient of smoking mixtures to relieve asthma and if smoked before bedtime, will bring about sound sleep. The flowers make a 'tea' which calms the nerves and encourages sleep. Pour 1 pt (570 ml) of boiling water on to a handful of flowers, strain and take hot or cold at bedtime. The same can be used as a tonic hair rinse. Remove the flowers when just open and it is the centre florets which provide the medicinal qualities.

The double flowered form is the best to grow for there is greater strength in their medicinal qualities and the flowers are produced with greater freedom. The variety Treneague bears no flowers but is a plant of very low habit and makes an excellent 'lawn' though it has no other uses.

CORSICAN THYME (*Mentha requienii*) In habit it more closely resembles the thymes than the mints and is also known as Spanish thyme being present in the Iberian Peninsula, across southern Europe and on several Mediterranean islands where it grows on mountainous slopes. It is a charming little plant forming a dense mat of dark green peppermint-scented leaves and is studded with tiny mauve flowers all summer. From the leaves, a pleasant 'tea' is made which will relieve indigestion and is warming to the stomach if taken hot on a cold day. Pour a pint of hot water on to a handful of leaves or tops and sweeten with a little honey.

It is an admirable plant for a path, spreading over the stones to form a rounded mat and it will release its scent when walked upon. Propagate by cuttings taken in July and inserted in sandy compost. Move to small pots when rooted and plant out in spring. A dry, well drained soil is essential and it may be included with the creeping thymes to make a fragrant 'lawn'.

MICROMERIA (*Micromeria cordata*)   Native of Corsica and southern Europe, it makes a spreading plant 4 in (10 cm) tall and is of shrubby habit, ideal to plant between paving stones. It has silvery-green heart-shaped leaves and in summer bears pale pink flowers in tiny spikes, to give it a heath-like appearance. The plant has the delicious scent of lemon thyme and is used in stuffings and to flavour soups and stews.

M. douglasii is of more prostrate habit and is the *herba buena* of California, the aromatic shoots being frequently used to flavour summer drinks when John Fothergill was 'mine host' at the sign of the Three Swans, Market Harborough. If used to make a 'lawn', the stems will root at the leaf nodes like ground ivy and this is the best way to propagate it. The leaves emit the refreshing smell of lemon verbena.

MOUNTAIN THYME (*Thymus serpyllum*)   A prostrate perennial differing from *T. drucei* (wild thyme) only in that its stems are covered in downy hairs and it is found only in the Brecklands of East Anglia, growing in sandy soil. It appears in an Anglo-Saxon manuscript as *serpulum* and its name, thyme, is derived from the Greek *thumos* (sacrificial smoke) for the plant was burnt during ancient sacrifices and later came to be burnt in places of worship for its pleasant odour. It also had much the same medicinal virtues as wild thyme, but in recent years, with the introduction of a number of handsome varieties, it has been grown mostly as a colourful paving plant. The type bears rosy-red flowers in neat terminal spikes and for contrast, albus bears white flowers and coccineus forms mats of deepest crimson when in bloom from June until August. Two lovely recent introductions are Pink Chintz which bears salmon-pink flowers and Bressingham Pink which possesses the additional value in that it blooms later than the others and extends the flowering season. The variety *lanuginosa* has its leaves, as well as its stems, covered with woolly hairs to give it a frosted appearance while the hybrid Lemon Curd has foliage which does smell like that favourite pie filling.

Of the other semi-prostrate thymes, all of which are delightful garden plants, *T. doerfleri* also has soft woolly foliage and bears pale pink flowers in June and July. Its foliage is pine-scented.

T. fragrantissimus has grey leaves which when pressed release the scent of orange peel as does *T. azoricus* which forms a mat of emerald green. *T. nitidus*, native of Sicily is a tiny grey-leaved thyme with the same pungency as the Common or Black thyme and *T. membranaceous*, native of Spain makes a rounded hummock of aromatic foliage and bears large clusters of white flowers. *T. herba-barona* is the baron of beef thyme, used to cook with roast beef in mediaeval times. It was rediscovered in Corsica by the late Mr Clarence Elliott who called it the seed cake thyme for its leaves when handled smell remarkably like caraway seeds. *T. comosus* is a tiny shrublet growing 3 in (7·5 cm) tall with lilac pink flowers and leaves which have the smell of turpentine.

The foliage of each of these dainty plants can be used in cooking for they add their distinctive flavours to meats and only a leaf or two are necessary to impart the scent. Several may also be included in *pot pourris*. They require a sandy soil and an open situation and are propagated from cuttings inserted into sandy compost. When rooted, grow on in small pots for the thymes do not take kindly to root disturbance and are best planted from pots with the soil ball intact.

PENNYROYAL (*Mentha pulegium*) There are two forms, one, *decumbens*, a prostrate perennial with oval-toothed leaves which release a powerful peppermint smell when pressed. When in bloom in August and September, it resembles the peppermint but in miniature, for it bears its pale reddish-pink flowers in whorls on 3 in (7·5 cm) stems. Another form, *erecta*, grows 6 in (15 cm) tall. Both forms are present about heathlands and on lower mountainous slopes in southern England and the Channel Isles but *decumbens* is more prolific. Gerard said it grew at 'Mile End, near London' and in his time it was sold in the streets of London to sweeten drinking water, while it would rid houses and ships of fleas. For this reason, Pliny named it *pulegium* because it was able to remove *pulices* (fleas) from beds and houses. The fresh herb would keep fleas away from the rush floor coverings of rooms, for which reason and because it released its minty scent when trodden upon, Tusser included it among the best of all herbs for strewing. The fresh plant bound on the forehead and temples will ease a headache and a 'tea' made by pouring 1 pt (570 ml) of hot water on to a handful of stems, will ease indigestion and, if taken at bedtime, acts as a carminative. It also reduces fever caused by a chill and if rubbed on to the face will keep away gnats and flies in summer.

But it was for stuffings that the plant was so widely used in earlier times, not only to counteract the greasiness and often unpleasant smell of meats when there was no refrigeration but when meat was expensive, as it usually was and is so today, stuffings or puddings as they were called, made the meat go further. Hence the plant came to be called 'pudding grass' for which purpose it was grown at Mitcham, Surrey (together with peppermint) on a commercial scale. As the flavour is strong, only a generous pinch of the dried or the finely chopped fresh herb should be used in stuffings, and if used for mint sauce, mix with it the milder apple mint. It may also be included in sausages and in sausage-meat made for Scotch eggs for it is an excellent compliment to all egg dishes.

Pennyroyal can be grown in a path or in a herbal 'lawn' or in the vegetable garden with the other mints for it has many uses. If growing in a 'lawn' do not plant too much of it, for it spreads rapidly. It is propagated by root division in autumn or spring and during the first summer, keep the soil comfortably moist. It may also be propagated by seed sown in boxes or in a frame in spring and planting out the seedlings when large enough to handle. For a 'lawn', the variety *decumbens* is the best.

WILD THYME (*Thymus drucei*) The wild or creeping thyme was well known to Shakespeare for it is found on the undulating Cotswold hills around his home town, and on the Sussex Downs and elsewhere, growing in open places and in a well drained calcareous soil to a height of about 4000 ft (1219 m). It will quickly form a spreading mat, its four-angled stems covered in tiny lance-shaped leaves and from June until September, bears tiny flowers of reddish-purple.

No plant is more often visited by bees and, when honey was held in high regard for sweetening and for making mead, hives were placed near wherever the plants grew in profusion. Edmund

Spenser wrote of 'the bees alluring thyme' and 'to smell of thyme' was an expression of greatest praise. The plant also had other uses and in the *Paradisus*, Parkinson wrote, 'There is no herb of more use in the houses of high and low ... for bathing, for strewing and to make sauces for fish and flesh'. Today, we use the common or upright thyme for culinary purposes, especially for stuffings, but wild thyme can be included in *pot pourris* and to scent a bath and may be used in the kitchen if the more pungent common thyme is not available.

Thymol, an essential oil obtained from the wild and common thyme has ten times the antiseptic powers of carbolic acid and is often employed medicinally. If a few thymol crystals are dropped in a jug of boiling water and the peppermint-scented steam is inhaled, it will quickly ease a sore throat or bring relief to a blocked nose caused by a cold in the head. And to make a cleansing lotion for body sores, dissolve five grains of thymol in 1 oz (28 g) of spirits of wine and 1 oz (28 g) of glycerine. To this add 6 oz (170 g) of water and shake up before applying with lint.

Oil of thyme is recommended for a nervous headache and is a restorative. A 'tea' made from an infusion of the leaves (fresh or dried) in 1 pt (570 ml) of boiling water and sweetened with a little honey will have the same effect. The tops boiled in white wine will, if taken a wineglassful at a time, be comforting to the stomach and will ease colic pains.

Wild thyme is propagated from the woody cuttings taken in July and inserted in a sandy compost. When rooted, move to small pots for the thymes resent root disturbance and plant out in spring.

Herbs for paths and 'lawns'

Herb	Botanical name	In bloom	Use
Baron of Beef thyme	*Thymus herba-barona*	June–Sept	To flavour beef
Calamint	*Calamintha ascendens*	July–Sept	For digestive troubles
Chamomile	*Anthemis nobilis*	June–Aug	Nervous complaints; hair tonic
Corsican thyme	*Mentha requienii*	June–Sept	For stomach upsets

Carpeting Herbs – To Make a Fragrant Path and Lawn

Herb	Botanical name	In bloom	Use
Micromeria	Micromeria cordata	June-Sept	To flavour soups and stews
Micromeria	Micromeria douglasii	June-Sept	To flavour drinks
Mountain thyme	Thymus serpyllum	June-Sept	Restorative
Pennyroyal	Mentha pulegium	Aug-Sept	For stuffings; carminative
Wild thyme	Thumus drucei	June-Sept	For stuffings; for inhaling

Dandelion and Chives

Herbs to Grow in the Kitchen Garden

In addition to those herbs that are most suited to planting in the flower border, shrubbery or herb garden, there are others which are of less attractive appearance or of coarser habit, some having a rootstock which, once established, makes it almost impossible to eradicate. Others, such as the mints, parsley, garlic and dandelion, on account of their habit and culture, are unsuitable for planting with those herbs growing in the border or shrubbery. The mints with their creeping underground rootstock will quickly spread over a wide area and crowd out other herbs growing with them so that they are better planted in beds to themselves. The mints and most of the other kitchen garden herbs require very different soil conditions from most of the other herbs, and are used in the kitchen rather than for medicinal purposes or for making 'teas' and tisanes (cold drinks in summertime) or for use in sweet bags and *pot pourris*. The kitchen garden herbs are mostly grown for their leaves which are used in salads or cooked to serve with meats either by boiling or steaming. There are others grown for their roots and these are described in the following chapter. They come into a separate category but they too, are plants of the kitchen garden, taking their place with other vegetable plants in the rotation of crops.

ALEXANDERS (*Smyrnium olusatrum*)   It is found near Alexandria in North Africa and may have reached England with the Romans who occupied that territory during Cleopatra's time. Long naturalised in Britain, on waste land near the eastern coastline of England and Scotland, and though really perennial, it is usually given annual or biennial treatment for it grows quickly. It grows 3–4 ft (1 m) tall with smooth furrowed stems and has glossy fern-like leaves, with toothed leaflets. It resembles Sweet Cicely, also in the myrrh-scent of its leaves and roots, both of which have been eaten by countrymen since earliest times. The leaves in early summer are, used sparingly, a welcome addition to a salad and also impart their flavour to soups and stews while the roots can be boiled in winter after lifting them in November and storing in boxes of sand; or leave them in the ground and lift when required.

The plant is best treated as biennial, seed being sown in July in drills made 16 in (40 cm) apart. An open situation is necessary and well drained soil. In early spring, thin the plants to 8 in (20 cm) apart in the rows and support them by extending twine along the rows held in place by canes or stakes. As the summer proceeds, earth up the plants at the base so as to blanch the tops of the roots and make them more tender when cooked. When the stems die back in autumn, cut away at ground level and lift the roots as required.

BUNCH ONIONS (*Allium fistulosum*)   Under this heading may be grouped the Welsh onion, Japanese bunch-onion, the Potato onion and the Tree onion, all plants of great hardiness which (with chives) can be used for flavouring soups and stews all the year round. They require a soil containing some humus to retain moisture in summer, otherwise ordinary garden loam will be suitable. They are deep-rooting plants so the soil should be well worked and the plants will benefit from a little decayed manure dug in at planting time. They will be happy in semi-shade but the taller growing Tree onion (*Allium cebe*) may be grown against a trellis or fence to which the stems are tied for they grow to 3 ft (about 1 m) tall. Or they, too, may be planted in beds and the stems allowed to fall over when the bulblets which cluster at the end of the stems like small shallots will take root in autumn and form a jungle of onions each of which will produce their clusters of six to a dozen bulblets the following year. Plant the bulblets in spring about 6 in (15 cm) apart if growing against a trellis, or 12 in (30 cm) apart in beds. They form their cluster of bulblets in summer and these are removed in autumn when dry and ripe. They are separated and kept in open boxes in an airy room to use during winter, in soups and stews, or they may be pickled to use with cold meats, or chopped and added to salads or used with cream cheese in sandwiches.

The Japanese bunch-onion (*A. fistulosum*) forms its onions in tight bunches of eight or nine at soil level. They are like small shallots and are harvested in the same way, lifting them when ripe in autumn, separating them and after drying, storing them in boxes in a frost free room. The variety Iwatsuki Green sends up long tender leaves, some of which can be used to flavour soups and stews after cutting into small pieces. Plant the bulblets about 10 in (25 cm) apart, merely pressing them into a firm soil (like shallots) with the tops uncovered.

The Welsh onion, native of Siberia, is like a small leek or large chive and grows in tufts. Like the chive, it can be planted at the edge of a path, 6 in (15 cm) apart. It is perennial and the onions are removed by lifting alternate roots of six or more onions and separating them. Replant one of them each time a clump is lifted and use the others in soups and stews after washing. The blanched lower stem and upper green leaf can be used.

The Potato onion (*A. ascalonicum*) resembles the shallot in size and shape, reaching golf ball size during summer if kept well supplied with moisture but unlike the shallot, which grows on the surface of the soil, the Potato onion grows beneath the soil, like potatoes. It is the mildest of all onions with a most pleasant flavour. The bulbs are treated like tulips and daffodils, planting them about 1 February if the ground is free of frost so that they can form a mass of roots before the warm spring sunshine starts them into growth. Plant them in an open sunny position 10 in (25 cm) apart and just below the surface. By early autumn they will be ready to lift, as for potatoes. Select a dry day with the soil as dry as possible and leave the bulbs on the surface for several hours to dry off. Shake away the soil and place on shelves or on a bench in an attic or shed to complete the drying and use through winter.

Keep several small bulbs for replanting in February. The larger bulbs can be boiled and served with white sauce when they are sweet and juicy, with a mild onion flavour.

CHIVES (*Allium schoenoprasum*)   It is one of the most useful of herbs and makes a delightful edging to a path or a bed of other herbs, growing 6 in (15 cm) tall and in summer it bears small pinkish-mauve flowers, like those of thrift, on leafless stems. It requires an open situation and a soil containing some humus. Plant the offsets 6 in (15 cm) apart and it increases by forming numerous offsets, clustered together like small spring onions. A perennial, it forms hollow rush-like leaves tapering to a point. The dark green leaves have a mild onion flavour and it is these that are used, cutting them off just above soil level and using them to flavour soups and stews and chopped finely, to scatter over scrambled eggs and a Welsh rarebit, also in salads and in cream cheese sandwiches. Like all members of the onion family, chives stimulate the appetite and lower blood pressure.

Chives are propagated by dividing the roots, gently 'teasing' apart the tiny onions and re-planting 6 in (15 cm) apart. Plant 1 in (2·5 cm) deep when the soil is moist but frost free. They may also be raised from seed sown in shallow drills (like spring onions) or in boxes in April and planting the seedlings in beds or as an edging. To keep the plants healthy and vigorous, give them an occasional mulch of decayed manure and sifted soil. The plants will continue to increase each year and may be divided in alternate years. Chives may also be grown in small pots in a sunny kitchen window, in a window box, or as an edging to a tub. They are both pretty and useful and are plants of extreme hardiness. Its ancient name was *seithes*.

DANDELION (*Taraxacum officinalis*)   In the lawn and flower garden it is an obnoxious and difficult weed to eradicate but when correctly grown in the kitchen garden it is a most valuable and health-giving plant to include in an early summer salad. It takes its name from its lion-toothed leaves, those of the cultivated form being larger and crisper than in the wild. The plant is a tonic and blood purifier and, in the Industrial North it is used with burdock for this purpose and to make a tonic beer to drink in summer.

The distilled water of the chopped leaves will reduce a temperature during a fever and will clear the kidneys of impurities. The roots, after drying and roasting, can be ground to a powder and mixed with coffee or used instead of that beverage. They have a similar flavour, act as a tonic and clear the kidneys. But it is the leaves, when blanched, that make a welcome addition to an early summer salad often before lettuce is ready.

Seed is sown early in spring in a deeply worked soil containing some humus and a little decayed manure. As the roots are blanched before the leaves are used in salads, the best method is to sow seed in circles of a size to enable the plants to be covered by a large plant pot. Scatter a few seeds in the circle of soil and rake them in. If six to eight circles are sown, this will enable several groups of plants to be blanched during one year and others the next year for, after removing the leaves from one group of plants in one year, they should be rested the next to allow the plants to recover. Or sow in squares of the size of a deep orange box which can alternatively be used to cover the plants. Thin the seedlings to 6 in (15 cm) apart and do no blanching (which is a type of forcing) until their second year but keep the plants watered in dry weather.

As soon as the plants begin to grow in spring and when the leaves are several inches high, cover them and within ten days, the leaves will have grown 6 in (15 cm) long and be crisp and pale green, without bitterness. Use them in salads from early April until the end of June or in sandwiches, with or as an alternative to lettuce. Then pull no more leaves that year.

GOOD KING HENRY (*Chenopodium bonus-henricus*) A perennial, growing 2 ft (60 cm) tall with arrow-shaped leaves which in olden days were applied as a poultice to body sores and they were also used to heal cuts and wounds sustained by carpenters or by those in combat. But today, it is grown for the young shoots which appear in spring when Brussels sprouts and curly kale have finished. If the plants are grown in rows made 16 in (40 cm) apart, they can be earthed up when new growth begins and this will partially blanch the shoots and make them sweet and tender. They are cut when about 6 in (15 cm) tall, peeled and boiled and served with melted butter to accompany meat or game. They taste like asparagus. Later in the year, the leaves can be removed and cooked like spinach.

Seed is sown in spring in shallow drills, the plants being thinned to 12 in (30 cm) apart in the rows. Keep watered in dry weather and do not cut any roots until the second year. Remove a few from each plant and let the others grow on. It cleanses the kidneys and acts as a gentle laxative.

LAMB'S LETTUCE (*Valerianella locusta*)   It is also known as Corn Salad for it grows in cornfields and about hedgerows and its leaves make a pleasant addition to an early summer salad. The leaves appear early, during April when lambs find them tasty. Long a favourite vegetable and salad crop in France, it was the Huguenot refugees who first drew our attention to its good qualities. A low-growing annual with oblong leaves, it is the young lower leaves which are used in salads for they are less palatable when they are old.

To maintain a supply, seed is sown in drills made 12 in (30 cm) apart, in late July and another sowing is made in April. Thin to 6 in (15 cm) in the rows and in winter cover those plants from a July sowing with cloches.

LOVAGE (*Ligusticum officinale* and *L. scoticum*)   Both the English lovage, *L. officinale* and the Scottish lovage *L. scoticum* may be native plants or the former may have come with the Romans for it grows in profusion about the cliffs of Liguria and along the Mediterranean Coast. *L. officinale* grows 3–4 ft (1 m) tall and has dark green leaves divided into narrow segments while *L. scoticum*, found on cliffs and rocky ground in North East England and in East Scotland, grows to about half the height and has polished emerald green leaves divided into broader segments. They have long parsnip-like tap roots and all parts of the plants have the celery flavour and smell. The plants are perennial but die down in winter, coming again in spring when the new shoots can be earthed up to partly blanch them. When 8 in (20 cm) tall, they are removed to grate raw into salads, or braised to serve with meats. The leaves can also be chopped and included in salads and will impart their celery flavour to soups and stews. All parts of the plant can be used, the stems being candied, like angelica, for decorating cakes and to eat as a sweetmeat. A decoction of the leaves, a handful to 1 pt (570 ml) of hot water, if used as a gargle, will ease a sore throat and if a small cupful is taken daily, it will relieve rheumatic pains.

The plants are perennial and with their polished leaves, bring distinction to a border but are usually grown in the kitchen garden where they can be earthed up more easily. The plants require a deeply worked soil containing some humus and a little decayed manure. Plant 20 in (50 cm) apart and propagate by dividing the long woody roots in autumn or spring as for rhubarb; or from seed sown in spring in drills made 20 in (50 cm) apart, thinning to 18 in (45 cm) apart in the rows. The seed must be fresh or it will not germinate well.

MARIGOLD (*Calendula officinalis*)   It is one of the most attractive plants of the herb garden and may be grown anywhere, in small beds where it will bloom all summer, in tubs and window boxes, at the front of a border and in the kitchen garden, where its flowers and leaves can be used through summer and autumn in the kitchen as well as to beautify the home. It received its botanical name because it is in bloom on the first day (the kalends) of almost every month of the year and it is dedicated to Our Lady being in bloom on all the festivals of the Virgin.

Native of southern Europe, and possibly introduced by the Romans, it has been a garden plant since earliest times for apart from its beauty, it had so many uses. An annual with a strongly pungent but not unpleasant smell, it grows 12 in (30 cm) tall and bushy. Seed is sown in drills or in boxes in spring and it germinates as quickly as mustard and cress. Established plants will also seed themselves each year. Plant in beds, setting the seedlings about 10 in (25 cm) apart and an open position is necessary though it is happy in ordinary soil. During the hard frosts, the plants will be killed but if a pinch of seed is sown in a pot(s) in June, they can be taken indoors in October and will continue to grow through winter. The best variety is the orange Radio with long quilled petals and its counterpart, Golden Beam.

Dr Hughes, practising in Brighton until the end of the 1920s, said that the plant was 'a precious vulnerary' which was used by surgeons during the American Civil War to heal battle wounds, using the juice of the flowers and leaves. Marigold water obtained from the flowers is soothing to the eyes and its essence is today being used more and more, in face creams for it makes the skin soft and white. Marigold 'tea' is soothing at bedtime and encourages sleep. It is made by pouring a pint of boiling water on to a handful of flowers and after five minutes, straining and taking a small wineglassful.

The plant is also grown for its culinary uses. The petals are scattered into summer salads and into broths and stews, to which they impart a pleasant bitterness. The petals can be dried and used in this way through winter and, until the end of the nineteenth century, were to be obtained at all grocers shops where they were kept in large wooden drums. For this reason, the plant has always been known as the 'pot' marigold for the flowers were included in all those pots cooking on a cottage fire. Gerard said that in his time, 'no broths were made without dried marigolds' and Tusser included it as one of his 'herbs for the kitchen'.

To dry the petals, cut off the flowers at the end of the stems and spread on trays in an airy, sunny room, turning them daily for two weeks. They will have become a deep golden-bronze yet still retain their unusual smell which is quite appetising. The petals are then pulled from the disc florets and placed in bags or boxes to use when required. It is only the fresh flower petals that are included in salads. After drying, they tend to be rubbery.

MINT (*Mentha spicata*, etc.) Among the most interesting of herbs are the mints which are best grown in the kitchen garden, in beds to themselves owing to their creeping rootstock for in a border, the plants are difficult to keep under control. Shakespeare knew of their many qualities and in 'A Winter's Tale', Perdita says:

> Here's flowers for you,
> Hot lavender, mints, savory, marjoram.

Here, the playwright coupled together all those most powerfully smelling herbs which had so many uses. Parkinson, living at the same time, describes three varieties of mint and says 'where docks

91

are not to hand, bruised mint leaves laid on any place stung by wasps or bees, is to good purpose' which is very true. There are at least thirty species and varieties of mint and as many as twenty or so may be obtained from most herb growers. Each is of interest and requires much the same culture; that is a soil enriched with some humus, such as decayed manure or used hops and they grow best in a semi-shaded situation, where the soil does not dry out too quickly. With their creeping rootstocks, mints will soon exhaust the soil if it is not given a top dressing each year, preferably in late autumn, of freshly riddled soil mixed with some decayed manure, old mushroom bed compost being ideal. The ground should be well limed for mint does not grow well in an acid soil.

The best method is to plant in trenches made 6 in (15 cm) deep and to the width of a spade. At the bottom put in a 2 in (5 cm) layer of decayed manure, then cover with 2 in (5 cm) of riddled soil over which the long straggling roots are spread out about 12 in (30 cm) apart. Then cover with 1 in (2·5 cm) of soil and water. Where growing commercially (and there is always a demand for fresh and dried mint), the roots are obtained from specialist growers by the bushel and are sent out in sacks. Take care not to expose them to wind when planting for this will cause them to shrivel and they will take some time to recover. If growing a number of varieties, plant each in a separate bed.

About 1 November is the best time to plant for the plants will then have started to die back and it is usual to cut back the stems at this time, before top dressing the beds. This is also the time to lift and divide the roots for re-planting. Quite small pieces will grow into a vigorous plant.

Keep the plants growing by watering them in dry weather and during their first year, remove only a few sprigs or stems. These should be cut off about 2 in (5 cm) above soil level when 6–8 in (15–20 cm) high, using scissors to do so. Where growing for market, make up into bunches of eight to ten stems and fasten together with a rubber band.

To keep the plants free from rust, which often attacks the stems and leaves as orange-coloured spores, making them unsaleable, it is advisable to immerse the roots in water heated to just 112°F (26°C) for 10 minutes before planting. You will then start with clean stock for, although the disease does not attack the underground roots, the spores may be present on the exposed crowns of the plants and will attack the stems when they begin to grow again. To keep the plants free from rust it is usual to make up fresh beds every four to five years, planting into fresh ground.

Forced mint is always in demand and the method is to lift the roots about 1 November and to replant them closely together, in deep boxes of soil. Keep the soil moist and in a temperature of 52°F (11°C) the shoots will have reached a height of 6 in (15 cm) within a month. There is no hurry to force them into growth for it is not until the new year that fresh mint sauce is needed to accompany the new season's lamb. If no heat is available, plant several roots in a frame and there will be young stems to cut by 1 March; or cover several roots where growing in the open, with a cloche and the mint will be ready at about the same time.

The mints may be divided into three groups: the culinary mints; medicinal mints; and the fragrant mints which are mostly used in *pot pourris* and to perfume bath water. Of the culinary mints, *M. rotundifolia*, the Round-leaf mint, of which the best form is Bowles' Variety, is that most suitable for mint sauce. But the connoisseur will make a mint sauce to suit his own palate by carefully mixing several culinary mints and making the sauces with best malt vinegar. Bowles' Variety is the most resistant to rust of all the mints. Another excellent variety is the Apple mint with its fresh scent of ripe apples which also makes a delicious sauce. Like Bowles' Variety, the stems grow to 20 in (50 cm) high. The true Apple mint has its leaves splashed with cream. With its delicate flavour, it is used by confectioners to flavour cakes.

Another culinary mint is Spearmint or Lamb Mint, *M. viridis* which is included with peas and new potatoes and is used to flavour chewing gum. It is a hairless mint growing 12 in (30 cm) tall with vivid green leaves which release a pungent minty smell when pressed. The lilac flowers are borne in handsome spires, hence its original name was spiremint. *M. cordifolia* with its large heart-shaped leaves is also excellent for mint sauce and has much of the spearmint flavour.

M sylvestris, the white or woolly mint, present in damp, open woodlands, is a handsome species and could be included at the front of a border with the silver-leaved *Stachys lanata*. With its distinctive flavour it, too, makes a delicious mint sauce which in mediaeval times was used to help the digestion of the often tough meats and also took away the rancid taste. Several of these mints are used in the manufacture of Crême de Menthe, a green liqueur which will settle a rich meal better than anything. Another fine mint is *M. longifolia,* so named because of its tall, upright habit rather like the woolly mint, its stems and leaves are silvered. A few leaves included with those of the other culinary mints, makes a delicious mint sauce.

Spearmint, placed in milk, will prevent it curdling in hot or thundery weather and an infusion of the leaves in hot water will relieve hiccoughs and flatulence and will 'warm' the stomach on a cold day.

To make a pleasant mint sauce, remove the leaves from the freshly gathered stems and chop finely. To every two dessert-spoonfuls of mint, give one of fine sugar and a small cupful of white wine and one of malt vinegar. Boil together the wine and vinegar with the sugar until the sugar has dissolved then remove from the stove and stir in the mint. Leave it for an hour or more until cold and pour into a screw-top jar to use as required. Mint sauce is best made in mid-summer when the mint is most potent.

Of the medicinal mints, Peppermint (*M. piperita*) is possibly a natural hybrid of spearmint and the water mint, *M. aquatica*. It grows about 15 in (38 cm) tall and has a hot, pungent smell. There are two forms, 'black' which is so called because the stems and upper surface of the leaves is purple-brown and in which the essential oil is more plentiful, and 'white', which has more deeply serrated leaves of bright green in which the oil is more refined. The plant was discovered in a field is Hertfordshire in 1700 and named and described by John Rea in his *Historia Plantarum* (1704). It was first grown commercially in Mitcham, Surrey about 1750 to provide peppermint oil for confectionary, Mitcham mint creams still being world famous. It was also grown for its ability to relieve sickness and nausea, for indigestion and when inhaled, to ease a hard cough and assist respiration. There is also a variety with handsome crinkled leaves, crispum.

The Japanese variety of our Cornmint, *M. arvensis*, known as *piperescens*, is that grown in the East for menthol, an antiseptic which, during the time of the Georgian kings of England, doctors and clergymen carried about in small silver boxes, to inhale the dried leaves and use as snuff, in times of pestilence. It has the penetrating smell of humbugs. Our native cornmint was used to sweeten water and to prevent milk curdling.

To warm the stomach on a cold day, *M. gentilis*, the Ginger mint, is recommended. It is a handsome mint with its dark leaves splashed with gold and its full name is *M. gentilis aurea variegata*. To make a winter drink, dry the leaves and pour 1 pt (570 ml) of boiling water on to a teaspoonful. Strain and sweeten with a little honey and drink hot. The fresh leaves can be used in summer.

Of the fragrant mints which are used to scent bath water and to include in *pot pourris*, *M. citrata*, the lemon mint is similar to the scent of lemon verbena. There are two varieties of it which should be grown in every garden, the pineapple mint which has green and gold foliage and when pressed, releases the scent of ripe pineapples; and the Eau-de-Cologne mint, which has the exact scent of the well known spirit.

Another mint with a delicious flavour is *M. aquatica*, the water or bergamot-scented mint and like the border plant of the same name, it makes a pleasing summer 'tea' taken hot with lemon juice and sweetened with a little sugar, or cold from the refrigerator, with a sprig of borage.

Nasturtium

NASTURTIUM (*Tropaeolum majus*)　A climbing annual with round (peltate) leaves and bearing brilliantly coloured flowers in shades of red, salmon and gold, the upper petal forming a long free spur.

It blooms from June to October and is native of Chile and Peru where it is used for food by the native peoples. Though in Britain it is chiefly grown for its multitudes of flowers and usually in hanging baskets and against a trellis, its leaves are rich in iron and sulphur and can be included in salads and cream cheese sand-wiches, imparting a pleasant bitterness which stimulates the appetite. The flowers, too, are edible and give interest to a salad while the seeds are pickled as an alternative to capers. Pick them when green and fill a screw-top jar with them. Then pour over them Tarragon vinegar which has been boiled with 1 oz (28 g) of salt and three or four peppercorns and allowed to cool. Leave in a dark cupboard for two months before using when they will make an excellent caper sauce to serve with fish.

The plant grows well in ordinary soil in a sunny situation. Plant the seeds in April 8 in (20 cm) apart on a wall, or in a window box on a terrace or verandah where the plants can drape themselves over the side and be ornamental as well as useful. Allow some seeds to mature and save these to plant next year.

PARSLEY (*Petroselinum crispum*) Named from petra (a rock) because it is found growing about rocky outcrops and cliffs in southern Europe and may have reached England during Tudor times. Turner, in his *Herbal* of 1548 wrote that he had seen it growing 'nowhere but in gardens'. With spinach, it is the richest in vitamin A of all plants whilst it is also rich in vitamins C and E as well as in iron and so should be on every table to sprinkle over egg dishes and fish as well as into soups and stews. It should be used fresh from the garden, finely chopped. It also makes an excellent sauce to accompany fish. Parlsey remains fresh when cut longer than any other plant and, with its crinkled emerald green leaves, is used in large quantities by hoteliers for garnishing and by fish merchants to make their slabs more attractive.

Parsley is a biennial (sown one year to use the next) and will usually remain fresh in the garden for two years from sowing time but to make sure of winter green, seeds can be sown in pots in spring and the plants taken indoors in November and placed in the kitchen window. Or the fern-like leaves may be frozen. Remove the leaves from the plants in summer when at their best, blanch them for two minutes in boiling water, then cool and drain off the water before placing in plastic bags and in the freezer.

Parsley requires a rich soil, containing some humus and decayed manure otherwise it will quickly go to seed in dry weather. Sow about 1 July in drills made 10 in (25 cm) apart and in a sunny position and make a sowing each year. There is a north country saying which believes that 'parsley goes nine times to the devil before it grows' and the seed takes longer than that of most other herbs to germinate. Always use fresh seed as old seed may not germinate at all. Keep the soil moist and the plants well supplied with moisture in summer. Begin to remove the leaves in spring and continue to do so until the following spring when new plants should be ready to take their place. Should the plants run to seed in summer, due to dry weather, clip them back to within 6 in (15 cm) of the base when the new leaves will appear. If the leaves are to be dried, place them on trays during June, in an airy room, preferably in full sunlight or in a low oven, repeatedly turning them until quite dry and this may take several days, even weeks. When quite crisp, rub down the leaves, remove the stalks and store in glass jars.

Covering a row of plants in early November with cloches will enable the leaves to stay green all winter if there is no freezer available.

The best variety is Champion Moss Curled which makes a plant of compact habit and bears thick curled fronds (leaves) of brightest green. For hardiness, Cluseed Dark Green Winter is recommended. Both can be sown as an edging to a path or bed or as an edging for a tub filled with other herbs. They may also be grown in a window box.

A teaspoonful of parsley seed infused in 1 pt (570 ml) of hot water is good for agues and fevers while a decoction of the roots, $\frac{1}{2}$ lb (225 g) to 1 pt (570 ml) of hot water and strained, will relieve painful kidney disorders caused by a chill.

SORREL (*Rumex acetosa*)   It is a tufted perennial growing 8–10 in (20–25 cm) tall with arrow-shaped leaves, the lower being short-stalked, the upper stem clasping. It is widespread on mountainous slopes and in hedgerows and is a valuable plant to grow in the garden for an infusion of the leaves makes an efficient gargle to ease a sore throat. Like those of Good King Henry, the leaves were bound over wounds and body sores to bring about rapid healing. A decoction of the leaves will reduce a temperature at times of fever. But it is as a restorative that it is now used, the leaves being rich in potassium salts. John Evelyn said 'it sharpened the appetite and gave so quickness to a salad, supplying the want of oranges and lemons, that it should never be omitted'. Use the young leaves in a salad or in cream cheese sandwiches and they can be boiled in a little water and used instead of spinach to place in omelettes.

Sorrel makes a delicious 'green' sauce to serve with rich meats such as duck and pork, to take away the greasiness. The recipe is given in a fourteenth-century manuscript in the Sloane Museum and it is made by pouring a little mint vinegar or white wine over a large handful of fresh leaves, beating to a fine consistency and adding a teaspoonful of sugar. It may also be served with boiled fish as it is in Ireland. In France, the leaves are included in soups to serve to travellers as a 'pick-me-up' after a long journey. The plant grown in France is *R. scutatus*, which is known as French sorrel and is the best to grow in gardens.

Seed is sown in spring in shallow drills made 10 in (25 cm) apart and thinning to 6 in (15 cm) in the rows. Ordinary soil is suitable if containing some humus and as it does not grow tall, it may be grown in pots, tubs or boxes in a courtyard or on a terrace for it remains green all the year. Use the leaves before they grow old.

SPINACH (*Spinacea oleracea*)   It is one of the richest sources of iron of all the vegetable kingdom and should be included in the diet of those who suffer from anaemia, though its unusual 'earthy' flavour when cooked is not to everyone's taste. The plant is also rich in chlorophyll which is able to raise the haemoglobin of the blood and so is a vital food for those who have suffered haemorrhage, while the fresh leaves have a higher vitamin A content than any other plant.

There is both summer and winter spinach. The former is grown from a succession of sowings made every three weeks from the end of March until late in July when a sowing is made of winter spinach. This will provide leaves the whole year round.

To prevent summer spinach running quickly to seed in dry weather, the soil should contain plenty of humus, including some decayed manure, and so that the plants will form as much leaf as possible, give the soil a sprinkling of nitrate of soda about 1 in (2·5 cm) away from the plants as soon as they have grown about 2 in (5 cm) tall.

Seed is sown in shallow drills made 10 in (25 cm) apart, thinning the plants to 6 in (15 cm) in the rows. Keep the plants watered in dry weather and begin using the old leaves when the plants are about 10 in (25 cm) high, steaming or simmering in a very little water or even in their own juice until tender. Remove the plants as soon as they run to seed for if other sowings have been made, there will be a succession of green through summer. It is the round leaf varieties that are sown in summer and of these, Cleanleaf which holds its leaves well above the ground and the strangely named Monstrous Viroflay with its large smooth leaves are among the most reliable. Both will be ready to begin using six to seven weeks after sowing and the leaves should be gathered just before they are to be used.

A sowing of winter spinach is made late in July and the hardiest is Bloomsdale Longstanding. It has large crinkled leaves held well above the ground and clear of wet soil which causes them to decay.

SUMMER SAVORY (*Satureia hortensis*) Native of southern Europe, it is an annual but is only half-hardy in Britain and should not be sown outdoors until mid-April in northerly gardens. But as it grows only 8 in (20 cm) tall, it can be sown and grown in pots in the kitchen window when seed is sown in early March. It has branching stems and oblong downy leaves which have a thyme-like flavour and are used in stuffings in summer when fresh and in winter when dried. If the plants are cut down early in autumn and strung up in an airy room (like sage), they will soon dry and can be used when required or rubbed down.

The first shoots will be ready in June with those broad beans sown in autumn and a sprig or two should be included with them. Also when finely chopped, the leaves are sprinkled over scrambled eggs or a Welsh rarebit and they are used in summer stuffings with sage or thyme.

Seed is sown in drills made 6 in (15 cm) apart thinning the seedlings to 4 in (10 cm) in the rows. Or scatter a few seeds in a pot of soil and place in a sunny window. If possible, use sterilised compost which is free from weed seeds.

Begin using the leaves when the plants are about 3 in (7·5 cm) high and any not used by early autumn are cut back to ground level to make into bunches to dry for winter use.

SWEET CICELY (*Myrrhis odorata*)   A handsome perennial which could find a place in any chapter in this book. It could be included in the border or grown as a root crop but for its many culinary qualities it is best grown in the kitchen garden. In the wild it is found from Lincolnshire northwards to central Scotland where it is the most common umbellifer. It prefers the cooler climes and is rare in the south. It grows 3–4 ft (1 m) tall with a hollow furrowed stem and has fern-like pinnate leaves which are grey-green and downy. They emit a pleasant myrrh-like scent when handled, a hot, spicy smell but when eaten taste sweet and sugary so that countrymen knew it also as Sweet Fern. The dark brown ridged fruits (seeds) also smell of myrrh.

Sweet Cicely is raised from seed sown in shallow drills in spring and thinning the plants to 2 ft (60 cm) apart. They require a well drained soil but with some humus in it to retain summer moisture. The plant will die back in winter but comes again in spring when the young leaves can be simmered like spinach and served with meats. They may also be included in salads, but sparingly for their flavour is pronounced. The roots are nutritious and may be grated raw into salads and served with salad oil, vinegar and seasoning, or boiled and served with white or cheese sauce. In olden times, they were candied, like eringoes (the roots of the sea holly) and enjoyed as a sweetmeat.

The plants should not be allowed to seed but if one stem on each is allowed to do so, the plants will seed themselves and main-tain a supply. The plants should not be lifted for their roots until two years old when they can be used in winter.

WATERCRESS (*Nasturtium aquaticum*)   Where there is fresh running water available, watercress can be grown and with spinach and parsley, it is the richest in iron of all plants and should be eaten by all who suffer from anaemia. Culpeper said, 'they that would live in health may eat watercress as they please' and it may be served with cold chicken and French fried potatoes as with lamb and new potatoes, in addition to including it in salads and with egg dishes, also in sandwiches with cream cheese. The plant is also rich in sulphur and is a blood purifier and the water in which the cut leaves and stems have been simmered, may be drunk daily to clear the complexion and also used to bathe the face to keep it free of blemishes.

A perennial plant, it grows 8 in (20 cm) tall and must have its underground stems immersed in water and in a mild climate it will grow all the year.

The plants are set out 3 in (7·5 cm) apart in beds made 6 ft (about 2 m) wide, with 4 in (10 cm) of water over the surface. Early summer is the time to make up the beds for they will then be established before winter.

If there is no running water, take out a trench 3–4 ft wide (1 m) and 12 in (30 cm) deep and at the bottom place a layer of decayed manure 4 in (10 cm) deep. This is covered with 3 in (7·5 cm) of soil, then the same depth of sand in which the plants are set out 6 in (15 cm) apart. They must be kept constantly watered when the weather is dry, leaving on the hose for thirty minutes at a time.

AMERICAN LAND CRESS (*Barbarea praecox*)   A biennial, it can be planted in a bed of moist soil and raised from seed sown in drills in spring or broadcast in a frame. The seed will germinate in three weeks if kept moist and three weeks later, the beds are made up. If the bed is covered with plastic in winter, the plants will continue to grow, except during very cold weather and they will continue to make growth throughout the following year. Erect a wooden frame around the bed, with boards held in place with wooden stakes and make a wooden light to the size of the frame using heavy gauge plastic sheeting instead of glass for the lights and there will be green to cut all winter.

WINTER SAVORY (*Satureia montana*)   In Greece where it abounds, it was believed to be a plant of the satyrs and it is present on mountainous slopes, being much in demand for flavouring foods. In Tudor times it was the most popular herb for stuffings, to accompany veal and venison. Michael Drayton, the Warwickshire poet, suggested using the dried leaves, with those of tansy, and mixed with breadcrumbs, 'to breade meate, be it fish or flesh, to give it a quicker relish' which is excellent advice. The plant was grown with thyme to form the knot beds of Tudor herb gardens for as Thomas Hyll said 'these endure all the winter through greene'. It is a perennial plant of neat, compact habit, growing about 10 in (25 cm) high, of woody habit, its small oblong leaves ending in sharp points. It requires an open, sunny situation and a well drained sandy soil, like the thymes, with which it grows in its native Greece. The leaves turn bronze in winter but still retain their fragrance which is warm and pleasing. The dried leaves are included in pork pies and sausages as well as in stuffings as an alternative to sage and thyme. The fresh leaves, mixed with parsley and finely chopped are sprinkled over fish and with basil are an ideal compliment for tomatoes, whether cooked or eaten raw.

A delicious butter to serve with fish is made by beating 4 oz (110 g) of butter to almost a cream and adding seasoning and a small teaspoonful of finely chopped savory. Place in the refrigerator for an hour before using.

Propagate by cuttings taken in June and inserted in pots or boxes of sandy soil. Keep moist and they will have rooted by the end of summer. Grow on in small pots during winter and plant out in spring 10 in (25 cm) apart. Plants can also be raised from seed sown in boxes in spring in a frame or sunny window. Transplant to small pots when large enough to handle and plant out the following spring. Winter savory can be grown in pots indoors or in a tub or window box.

Herbs used in the kitchen garden

Herb	Botanical name	When available	Use
Alexanders	*Smyrnium olusatrum*	Summer	As vegetable
Bunch onion	*Allium fistulosum*	All year	Flavouring

Herb	Botanical name	When available	Use
Chives	*Allium schoeno-prasum*	Summer	In salads
Dandelion	*Taraxacum officinalis*	Summer	In salads
Good King Henry	*Chenopodium bonus-henricus*	Summer	As vegetable
Lamb's Lettuce (Corn salad)	*Valerianella locusta*	Summer	As vegetable
Lovage, English	*Ligusticum officinale*	Summer	As vegetable
Lovage, Scottish	*Ligusticum scoticum*	Summer	As vegetable
Marigold	*Calendula officinalis*	All year	Flavouring
Mint	*Mentha spicata*, etc.	All year	Sauces
Parsley	*Petroselinum crispum*	All year	All purposes
Potato onion	*Allium ascalonicum*	Winter	Flavouring
Sorrel	*Rumex acetosa*	Summer	As vegetable
Spinach	*Spinacea oleracea*	Summer	As vegetable
Summer Savory	*Satureia hortensis*	Summer	Stuffings
Sweet Cicely	*Myrrhis odorata*	Summer	As vegetable
Tree onion	*Allium cebe*	Winter	Flavouring
Watercress	*Nasturtium aquaticum*	All year	In salads
Winter Savory	*Satureia montana*	All year	Stuffings

Garlic

Root Herbs

Those herbs grown for the edible qualities of their roots and to a lesser extent their foliage, may also be classed as vegetable-herbs for in most instances the roots may be used for their food value as well as for their flavouring properties. Forming the most important part of the plant beneath the ground, they possess little or no beauty and, with one or two exceptions, are not suitable for growing in the border or with those herbs valued for their leaves or flowers. They also require very different soil conditions, a deeply dug soil well enriched with humus. This is needed to supply the roots with considerable amounts of moisture which makes up a large percentage of the edible root. The plants will make little growth in the dry, sandy soil, which most of the other herbs, with the exception of the mints, find greatly to their liking. The root herbs should be grown under the rotational cropping system together with other plants of the kitchen garden and so find no place in the garden devoted entirely to herbs. They are, however, so useful, especially for providing winter food that they should find a place in every garden. Being of compact habit, they may be grown where space is limited, even where the summer vegetables of more untidy habit have to be omitted. The root herbs are, in fact, among the most valuable plants of the garden, being extremely hardy and available over a long period, whereas many of the 'green' vegetables quickly run to seed before they can be used. Vegetables to last through the winter may be grown from only a very small piece of ground for the minimum of expense and trouble.

Preparing the ground

The root herbs require a humus laden soil though large quantities of manure are not necessary. Well nourished ground, able to retain moisture during the dry summer periods must be provided to enable the roots to make growth without any check. They will then grow to a good size and be sweet and succulent, devoid of any stringiness or bitterness as will be the case where they are lacking moisture. The ground should also be deeply dug, for several of the herbs are deep rooting, while the soil for all root crops should be brought into as fine a tilth as possible to prevent the roots becoming forked, or mis-shapen. Though root herbs will grow well in either a light or heavy soil, it will be advisable to trench in both cases so that heavy land may be better drained and light land may be made more retentive of moisture. It will also enable the soil to be brought to a fine tilth to as great a depth as possible.

First, give the ground a liberal dressing with lime, for root crops do not enjoy acid conditions, then take out a trench to a depth of about 15 in (38 cm). To the bottom add a layer of decayed farmyard manure or material from the compost heap and cover with soil. Then into the top soil removed from the next trench, incorporate some hop manure, shoddy, seaweed or peat and use this for filling in the first trench. The work should continue until the whole area of ground has been treated. It should then be allowed several days to consolidate before the seed is sown generally where the crops are to mature.

Harvesting roots

Those gardening in the south and west may leave the roots in the ground all winter, lifting them as required. In this way they will better retain their qualities, but elsewhere it will be better

105

to lift the roots in late autumn, late in October or early November so that they will not be harmed by severe frost which would also prevent them from being lifted when required. They are best lifted when the ground is in a friable condition. Press the garden fork well down and a few inches away from the plants which will have begun to die back early in autumn. Remove the foliage after lifting (that of Hamburg Parsley will remain fresh all winter if the roots are left in the ground) prising the roots upwards, and carefully knock away the soil taking care not to damage the roots. Place the roots in deep boxes and cover with sand or peat to exclude frost and prevent the roots shrivelling and place in a cellar, shed or outhouse, away from hot water pipes which will cause the roots to dry out and so lose quality. With a good stock of roots, apples and potatoes to last through the winter, one should never go hungry no matter how severe the weather while a cupboard filled with dry herbs will provide health giving drinks and herbs for flavouring all winter.

CELERIAC (*Apium graveolens* var. *rapaceum*)   Where celery proves difficult to grow, then celeriac should be substituted, for it grows quite easily if given a long season, which means raising the plants over a gentle hot-bed or in a greenhouse or frame or under cloches early in spring. The seed should be sown early in March, keeping the frame closed, and admitting air only if the spring sun is powerful. The seed should be kept comfortably moist when it will germinate by the month end, and be ready for transplanting into a cold frame in April. Never allow the young plants to lack moisture, and they are planted out during the last days of May.

Celeriac is planted on the flat, and needs far less attention in its culture than celery. It requires no blanching, no earthing up, neither so rich a soil nor so much moisture, but it does like a deeply dug soil into which is incorporated some humus in the form of peat and decayed manure, and while it does need some moisture, it does not need the copious amounts required by the celery.

The plants are set out 12 in (30 cm) apart each way, with the slight bulbous-like root just sitting on the top of the soil. Watering will be necessary to start the plants, then apart from keeping the ground free from weeds and the soil away from the root, which will grow half out of the ground, little more attention will be required. Towards the end of September soil should be scraped away from the roots, and any lateral shoots removed with a sharp knife.

In the south the roots may be left in the ground throughout the winter and used when required. In this way they will retain their strong celery flavour and nuttiness to a considerable degree. In the north the roots should be lifted early in November, the tops being removed and the roots trimmed. They will store through winter in boxes of sand in any shed or building.

The roots may be grated and used in a winter salad, or the sliced root may be fried in butter. Or again, it may be stewed and served with cheese or parsley sauce. The roots should be peeled before cooking. The variety to grow is Giant Prague.

CHICORY (*Chicorium intybus*)   Also called Succory, it is always expensive to buy, yet how easy it is to grow. It is the blanching which may put people off, though nothing could be easier. In fact, taking it right through from the moment the seed is sown, no vegetable is more easily managed. It is not really a root crop but the root is the all-important part of its culture.

Seed is sown in a rich soil early in June, not before, or the plants will run to seed in a dry, hot summer. Sow in rows 16 in (40 cm) apart and thin out the plants to 10 in (25 cm) apart in the rows when large enough. Being deep rooting plants, a deeply dug bed, to which considerable quantities of decayed compost and manure are dug in, is essential. Throughout summer the plants must be kept free from weeds and comfortably moist. So far, so good.

By the beginning of November the foliage will have died down, and the roots which by then will be about as thick as one's wrist may be dug up with care, trimmed of any small shoots and forced, a process which presents no trouble. A cellar, cupboard, garden shed or barn are all suitable places for the forcing or blanching, but very slight warmth is desirable to bring on the shoots in two or three weeks. An excellent method is to fill a large orange box with freshly composted manure to a depth of 6 in (15 cm) and over this is placed 6 in (15 cm) of fine loam. Remove all leaves just above the crowns and set the roots close together. Water thoroughly, and place in a completely darkened room. Or cover with sacking to exclude the light. With the slight heat from the compost the shoots will be ready for using in a fortnight, being broken off when about 8 in (20 cm) long, the roots being left undisturbed to bear a second lot of smaller shoots equally succulent. If the roots are to be forced in a kitchen cupboard, the manure will not be necessary, the other requirements being the same.

The shoots should not be removed until actually required for cooking, it requiring but a few minutes to prepare.

The variety to grow for cooking and to use in salads is Giant Witloof, which is tender and white when forced. The variety Brunswick, is only grown for its roots, which are dried and blended with coffee.

An infusion of the leaves in summer and applied to the face, will clear up any blemishes and the leaves added to broths and stews will sustain those recovering from illness. From the blue flowers, a water is obtained which if used to bathe the eyes will remove any tiredness or soreness.

But it is as a winter vegetable that it is mostly used. The forced roots are grated into salads, perhaps with celery, while when cooked, they make a delicious winter delicacy to accompany meats and game. After cutting or pulling away the shoot, cover with salt water for five minutes then remove and place in a casserole, cover with butter and season and cook slowly for an hour until tender.

FINNOCHIO (*Foeniculum vulgare* var: *dulce*) Famous in Italy as Florence fennel and elsewhere as Sweet fennel, it is to fennel as Hamburg parsley is to parsley, a swollen stemmed or rooted form which has attractions as a vegetable. The swollen stem is grated raw into a salad or boiled and served with white sauce to accompany meats. The leaves too, can be included in salads, also in soups and stews, to which they impart a sweet aromatic flavour, rather like celery. Parkinson, writing in the *Paradisus* said, 'Italians take much delight in the use thereof and transplant and whiten it to make it more tender. . . .' This alludes to the method by which soil is drawn up to the bulbous stems to blanch them as they increase in size, sometimes reaching the size of a small football and at least attaining tennis ball size if given plenty of moisture in summer. When of this size they are most tender and should be used.

Finnochio is an annual and seed is sown in shallow drills in spring, thinning to 8 in (20 cm) apart. A rich soil is required and an open, sunny situation. Begin earthing up the base of the stems when they reach golf ball size and keep the flower heads removed. Some leaves can be used through summer and when ready, stew or steam the swollen bases after removing the roots and upper stem or they can be fried. When cooked, they look much like onions.

A new variety, 'Perfection' is ready to use early August from an early spring sowing while the flavour is outstanding. It grows only 12 in (30 cm) tall.

GARLIC (*Allium sativum*)   It was Chaucer who wrote, 'Well loved he Garleck, Onyouns and the Leeke' and in his time, these highly flavoured plants were grown in every garden. Rich in alkaline salts and sulphur compounds, garlic is a blood purifier and splendid at warding off the common cold if regularly eaten during winter, the garlic has long been recognised as an aid to winter health. A writer of the early seventeenth century, relating the Great Frost of January 1608 said, 'our apothecary's shop is a garden full of herbs, our doctor a good clove of garlic', and well might we take counsel from this, and make a planting in the hope that the summer is kind enough to mature our crop. An ideal year for growing garlic was 1976, for the warm, dry weather persisted into October, allowing the crop ample time to mature. Garlic is sustaining and many a pilgrim would carry a clove or two to nibble on the journey to Canterbury.

Garlic requires a loose, sandy soil, a position of full sun, and neither humus nor manures. In the south two plantings are made, one towards the end of October, another in March, the latter being the most suitable time for planting in the north. The cloves as the segments of the bulbs are called, should be separated and planted in clean ground setting them out in drills 12 in (30 cm) wide, and spacing the cloves 6 in (15 cm) apart in the rows. They should be planted 2 in (5 cm) deep in a loose soil, this being one of the few plants that likes such a soil.

Cloves planted in October will, in a favourable district, be ready for lifting late in July, or before if it is required; those planted in March, being ready in the autumn. The plants should be lifted as soon as the leaves turn yellow, the bulbs being dried on the ground if the soil is dry, or else in an open shed. The bulbs are then strung together and hung up in a dry, frost-proof room for use when required.

HAMBURG PARSLEY (*Petroselinum crispum* var: *tuberosum*)   This is a root crop and so named on account of its likeness to raw parsley when cooked. It is in fact a turnip-rooted parsley and in addition its foliage, which also has a similar flavour to parsley, remains green throughout winter and so may be used for flavouring soups and to garnish fish, in place of parsley. The roots are grown in exactly the same way as parsnips and nothing could be easier. The seedlings will also transplant more readily than any other root crop.

The plants like a long growing season, sowing the seed in March in a soil previously manured for another crop. Bring to a fine tilth and sow thinly in rows 16 in (40 cm) apart, thinning out the young plants to 8 in (20 cm) apart. A second sowing should be made in June for maturing early the following spring so that there will be available an all year round supply. Throughout the summer never allow the plants to suffer from lack of moisture or the roots will grow woody and lack flavour.

The roots may be lifted at any time during winter and early spring, with those roots from a later sowing ready early the following summer. Like parsnips, the Hamburg parsley may be cooked in numerous ways, none being more appetising than when fried in butter. The roots and foliage may also be used grated and shredded in salads throughout the year.

HORSERADISH (*Armoracia rusticana*)   It is the roots that have medicinal and culinary uses and as it is so difficult to eradicate when once established, it should be confined to an out-of-the-way corner of the garden where it may grow rampant. It is perennial and forms large bright green leaves and equally large tap roots which are marketed in bundles of a dozen or so roots, trimmed

110

Horseradish

to the same length but of various thicknesses. It is as good for the kidneys and bladder as asparagus and barley, while no beef may be enjoyed to the full without its horseradish sauce. This is made by grating 1 oz (28 g) of the scraped roots and mixing with a teaspoonful of sugar and a little malt vinegar. Season and stir in $\frac{1}{2}$ pt (275 ml) of cream and place in the refrigerator until required.

Seed is sown in early spring, the plants being thinned to 12 in (30 cm) apart in the rows while it may also be propagated by replanting the small roots in autumn when some of the plants are lifted to make sauce.

RAMPION (*Campanula rapunculus*)   A member of the campanula family, it is one of our most beautiful wild flowers, growing to a height of 3 ft (1 m) or more and present on chalky outcrops of southern England. It is a plant more for the herbaceous border than the vegetable garden, where its large spires of white or purple bells gives it a most stately appearance. But it is mostly grown with the vegetables for its roots which may be grated raw into a winter salad or braised, to serve with meat and game. The roots have an agreeable nutty taste. The leaves may also be used in salads or cooked like spinach.

Seed is sown in early April, in drills made 8 in (20 cm) apart,

111

where the plants are to be grown for their roots, thinning them to 4 in (10 cm) apart in the rows. They can be used when young and quite small, in their first winter if sown early, and from then onwards until they have become large and coarse for which reason it is advisable to make a sowing in alternate years.

When grown in the flower border, it is the leaves which are used for in addition to their food value, they make an excellent water for the complexion.

SALSIFY (*Tragopogon porrifolius*)   Known as the 'vegetable oyster' because of its unique and delicate flavour, it is also a valuable diuretic. The roots grow to about 8 in (20 cm) long and are about 1 in (2·5 cm) in diameter at the shoulder, tapering slightly to the end. They must be lifted with care for if they break, they 'bleed' and flavour is lost. For the same reason they must not be peeled. Scrape lightly and boil until tender, using the liquid to make a white sauce to serve with them. After scraping the roots, place in a bowl of cold water and add a little lemon juice to preserve their whiteness after cooking. The roots are transferred from the bowl to the saucepan just before they are to be boiled or they are delicious baked and served with cheese sauce. Seed is sown in soil which has been manured for a previous crop; in a too rich soil, the roots will 'fork'. Sow early April in shallow drills made 8 in (20 cm) apart and thin to 6 in (15 cm) in the rows. Begin lifting the roots about 1 November and use through winter, though in the north, it is advisable to lift the entire crop in November and store in boxes of sand.

SCORZONERA (*Scorzonera hispanica*)   Native of the Iberian Penin-sula, it was Louis XIV, plagued so much by indigestion, who ordered this root to be grown in large quantities in the Royal Gardens at Versailles. For those who also suffer from this trouble, this is an important vegetable to grow with a flavour quite as pronounced as that of the salsify. But like that vegetable it will also 'bleed' and lose its flavour if carelessly lifted, or if cut exces-sively before it is cooked. In our campaign for kitchen cleanliness it has fallen from the favour it enjoyed during the eighteenth century, when kitchen maids were readily available for its cleaning, its almost black skin adversely affecting its many good qualities.

The plant requires exactly the same culture as salsify, a long growing season and a deep, friable soil. It may be lifted at any time during winter, and even left in the ground to be used in early spring when there is often a shortage of vegetables. The best variety is Giant Russian.

SKIRRET (*Sium sisarum*)   This is a perennial root plant, the roots being lifted as required for cooking, the small ones being replanted to grow on the following year. Alternatively, several plants may be left untouched until early spring when they are lifted, divided and replanted. Though the roots, like year old dahlia tubers, are most delicious cooked in butter during winter, skirret is now rarely grown. The plant grows 2 ft (60 cm) tall and has white flowers, like those of parsley. The long, thin tuberous roots which form in bunches, like the fingers of the hand, are peeled and baked in butter and possess a sweet, parsnip-like flavour. Water from boiled skirret roots is excellent for the kidneys.

WINTER RADISH (*Raphanus sativus*)   Few have heard of the Black Winter radish let alone grown it, yet it was a winter vegetable well known to Tudor and Stuart gardeners. Parkinson describes its qualities and admirably sums up its culture when he says, 'the Black Radishes are most used in the winter and must be sown after midsummer; if sown earlier they would run up to stalk and seed'. Indeed they do, and sowing takes place towards the end of July, the seed being sown in drills 10 in (25 cm) apart in a soil which has been well manured for a previous crop.

In Parkinson's *Paradisus* (1629) this radish is illustrated, and is shown as a round root, almost like a small turnip. It is completely black skinned, but the flesh is white and succulent if grown well, being in no way stringy. Sliced or grated into a salad after removing the skin, it has a distinct nutty flavour, without any of that 'fieriness' found so often in summer radishes.

The seedlings should be thinned out to 6 in (15 cm) in the rows, kept free of weeds and well watered through late summer. In late October the roots are lifted and should be stored in a cellar or cool shed in dry sand to be used through the winter. They are delicious used as *hors d'oeuvre* when they should be sliced and served with salad oil. There is also a long form, also quite black

113

and also grown by Tudor gardeners. It requires the same culture but is not quite so satisfactory, if the soil is heavy or stony, as the round variety. It was consumed in quantity in olden times as it was considered an excellent cure for bladder troubles.

Those who are put off by the appearance of the Black Radish should grow the handsome China Rose radish. It requires the same culture in every way, being sown in July in drills and lifted and stored in the same way. In appearance it is like a large French Breakfast, almost of blunt tubular form, thickening towards the base. The colour is vivid cerise-red with the flesh white, cool and crisp. It is most attractive sliced with the black radish and used for *hors d'oeuvre* or salads. It is also delicious for winter sandwiches served with Land Cress, or with cheese and brown bread.

Herbs to grow as root crops

Herb	Botanical name	When available	Use
Celeriac	*Apium graveolens* var. *rapaceum*	Winter	Flavouring As vegetable
Chicory (Succory)	*Chicorium intybus*	Winter	As vegetable
Finnochio (Sweet Fennel)	*Foeniculum vulgare* var. *dulce*	Summer	As vegetable In salads
Garlic	*Allium sativum*	Winter	Flavouring and Medicinal uses
Hamburg Parsley	*Petroselinum crispum* var. *tuberosum*	Winter	As vegetable
Horseradish	*Armoracia rusticana*	All year	Sauces
Rampion	*Campanula rapunculus*	All year	As vegetable
Salsify	*Tragopogon porrifolius*	Winter	As vegetable
Scorzonera	*Scorzonera hispanica*	Winter	As vegetable
Skirret	*Sium sisarum*	Winter	As vegetable
Winter radish	*Raphanus sativus*	Winter	In salads

Borage

Annual and Biennial Herbs

There are a number of herbs valued for their medicinal and culinary virtues which are annual or biennial plants. An annual is sown and matures in the same year, being sown sometime in spring, depending upon its hardiness, while a biennial is sown the year before that in which it reaches maturity, usually in July or August, so that the plants will be established before winter. Among these plants are many grown for their aromatic seeds most of which, in the British Isles, require as long a growing season as possible to ripen and these plants are given biennial treatment, sowing late the previous summer and if the garden is exposed to cold winds, covering with cloches to get them through the winter. Many of the plants have a beauty which suggests their being grown in the flower or herb border, as indeed they can be, plants such as borage with its brilliant blue flowers and marigold, while others such as coriander and chervil have attractive foliage. They are plants of various heights and can be sown among those perennials which occupy a permanent place in the border; or they may be sown in the kitchen garden, together with those plants that are grown mostly for their food value.

Annuals and biennials are inexpensive, the seed costing only a few pence and they grow quickly, some reaching maturity within six months so that they can be used soon after they are sown.

As a general rule, seed is sown in the open ground early in spring where the plants are to mature for most of them do not transplant readily. Among the few exceptions are marigold and borage. Also, as those plants grown as annuals have only a few months to grow before they begin to die back, transplanting would delay their growth and in a summer of adverse weather those herbs grown for their aromatic seeds would not have sufficient time to ripen them. For this reason, those which can be treated as biennials should be, for they will have longer to mature. This however, depends upon soil and climate. In a heavy soil, few biennials will survive a wet winter, nor will they have as much chance of success if grown as biennials north of the Humber as they would, south of this line unless the plants can be covered with cloches in winter.

Sowing the seed

Biennials are sown in July or early August, to enable them to become established before winter. Also, as this is usually the warmest time of the year in the British Isles, germination is rapid and there are few seeds which do not produce a plant. If they can be safely brought through the winter, the plants will get away to a good start with the warmer spring weather and will be at least a month in advance of those sown in spring which is often a cold time of the year. If so, germination will be delayed if seed is sown in spring. For this reason it is advisable to sow as soon as weather and soil conditions permit and if the early sowings can be covered with cloches removed from the biennials, this will hasten germination. The cloches should be in position at least ten days before the seed is sown so as to warm the soil. If growing in the vegetable garden, sow in drills (rows); if in the border, sow between established herbs of perennial habit. Sow in small groups and cover with a barn or tent cloche and fix a piece of glass at each end to exclude cold winds. But no seeds can be sown until the soil is clear of frost and it has begun to dry out and warm up after winter. This may be towards the end of March in the south; early April in the north. There is usually a difference of a month in sowing times between the most southerly and most northerly gardens of Britain so that annual and biennial herbs do better in the warmer parts, especially those grown for their seeds. These are used for flavouring culinary dishes and also for medicinal purposes. They can be stored easily, and will keep for some time without deteriorating, but will ripen fully in Britain only in a long warm summer and when treated as biennials. To enable them to obtain as much sun as possible, sow in an open situation.

Among the annual herbs are some which are less hardy than others and must not be sown too early, not until the frosts have finished. Among these herbs is the sweet or knotted marjoram and summer savory, also sweet basil which in Britain is usually given annual culture. These are plants of southern Europe and may be killed by a late frost if sown too early. They should not be sown until the end of April unless sown in pots or boxes in a frame or sunny window for these herbs will readily transplant. They are best sown under glass.

Annual herbs require a well drained soil but one containing some humus to retain summer moisture or growth will be slow and stunted. Biennials which occupy the ground through winter, require a soil that is particularly well drained or the plants will damp off. Apart from these considerations, ordinary soil is suitable for the plants occupy the ground for no more than fifteen months if treated as biennials and for less than half the time where grown as annuals. Clean ground is necessary for if the plants are in competition with an abundance of weeds, they will make little growth. The soil, too, must be brought to a fine tilth before the seed is sown. Remove any large stones and work in some humus to a depth of at least 10 in (25 cm) for many annual herbs are deep rooting. To provide humus, material from the garden compost heap such as decayed greens, tea leaves and old newspapers is suitable; or dig in some decayed leaves or spent hops which are readily available from a local brewery. Farmyard manure must not be used, especially for those herbs grown for their seeds and which produce a larger number of seeds where the soil is starved of plant food but is not lacking humus to hold moisture in dry weather. Even so, the hotter the summer, the better will the seeds mature and the more potent will they be.

Sowing the seed

Select a day when the soil is reasonably dry and friable so that it will not stick to the boots when walked upon and when a strong wind is not blowing for the seed is usually light and readily blown away. A strong wind makes sowing in drills most difficult. If sowing in the border, mark the places where the seed is to be sown with a label on which the name is printed and make sure to sow the taller growing herbs to the back and the most dwarf to the front. Scatter a pinch of seed over an area of about 1 sq ft (930 sq cm) and rake it into the surface, putting a cloche in position if one is available; or sow the seed in a circular drill made with the rim of a bucket.

If sowing in drills in the kitchen garden, make the drills north to south, using the back of a rake and make them 1 in (2·5 cm) deep. Use a garden line to keep the drills straight. Sow thinly, a pinch at a time, then cover with soil and rake the surface level. Be sure to mark each drill with a cane or label with the name of the herb on it. If the soil is dry, water the drills and do so whenever necessary to keep the seed moist or germination will be slow. When the seedlings are large enough to handle, thin to the required distance apart but biennials sown in late summer are best left until April. Where cloches are available, cover the rows in November before the first frosts and remove the cloches about 1 April. As the plants make growth, it is advisable to insert a few twiggy sticks along the rows to give them support and those which grow tall should be supported by strong twine held in place by strong canes.

Those annuals growing in a border should be left until the end of autumn before removing them, to enable them to seed themselves. The seedlings will appear in spring around where the plants were growing. The old plants should be placed on the compost heap. Those grown for their seed will have the stems removed in early autumn or as soon as the seed pods begin to open and before the seed is shed. Inspect the plants daily and when dry, cut off the heads and place each herb in a cardboard box. Move to an airy room and spread out on sheets of brown paper to dry. When so, remove the seeds from the heads and place in glass jars or boxes to use as required. Do not forget to name each one.

Annual and biennial herbs

Those grown for their seed(s):

ALKANET (*Anchusa officinalis*) Common alkanet is a biennial growing 18 in (45 cm) tall, with ovate leaves and bearing purple-blue flowers from May to August in short axilliary spires. A garden plant naturalised on and around old buildings especially in Kent and Sussex, Evelyn suggested using it as a restorative, like borage, for it contains nitrate of potash in similar quantity. It is also astringent and an infusion of the flowers in hot water will help in cases of dysentery and diarrhoea. It makes a pleasant summer drink and the flowers and leaves give a cool, cucumber flavour (also like borage) to drinks and are attractive when used in salads.

Seed is sown in July and thin or transplant the seedlings to 12 in (30 cm) apart. As with all biennials, take care not to dig them up when tidying the border in late autumn. It enjoys a dry, sandy soil and a sunny situation.

ANISE (*Pimpinella anisum*) A half-hardy annual, native of northern Africa and the Near East, it requires an above average summer in Britain to ripen its seed hence it is mostly confined to Essex and East Anglia. Even so, it is well worth growing in warmer parts for the leaves are handsome and have the unique aniseed flavour. A few leaves add interest to a salad. A favourite plant of olden times, the essential oil from its seed was effective against lice when rubbed into the hair or on to the body and from its seed, aniseed 'balls' were made, coated in sugar for children to suck. The plant grows 18 in (45 cm) tall with finely serrated leaves, like ferns and bears white star-like flowers followed by large round seeds. Today, most of the seed is imported from India and northern Africa and the oil obtained from the seed, is used in cough mixtures. To relieve bronchitis or a hard cough, infuse 1 oz (28 g) of seed in 1 pt (570 ml) of boiling water and collect the oil which rises to the top. Mix one part to four parts spirits of wine and take six drops in a tablespoon of hot water.

For flatulence or to settle the stomach at bedtime, take a small cupful of aniseed 'tea'. This is made by pouring a cupful of hot water on a teaspoonful of seed.

BORAGE (*Borago officinalis*) An annual or biennial, growing 16 in (40 cm) tall, it should be grown in every border if only for its brilliant blue flowers, the anthers meeting to form a jet black cone at the centre. In bloom July and August, it is much visited by bees and although the flowers are not scented, the stems and leaves when broken, release a cool cucumber flavour so that a sprig included in summer drinks, cider especially, imparts a refreshing, 'quick' taste. Gerard said that 'the leaves and flowers put into wine, makes men and women glad and merry' as indeed it does for the juice is rich in nitrate of potash, a natural restorative and invigorator. One of the Cordial flowers, the distilled water 'comforts the heart' and the flowers add beauty and flavour to salads. They are also candied, like violets, to use in confectionery.

To maintain a supply, seed is sown in July and again in April, directly into the border or into boxes, transplanting the seedlings to 16 in (40 cm) apart. If the soil is undisturbed, it will readily seed itself.

BURDOCK (*Arctium lappa*) A biennial growing 3–4 ft (1 m) tall, it is an obnoxious weed in the garden with a long deep tap root which exhausts the soil. It has large wavy heart-shaped leaves and bears thistle-like flower heads in loose corymbs. The involucre forms a ball of hooked spines which stick to the clothes when thrown by children. As a blood purifier it has no equal and for this purpose it is grown commercially in USA. It is the root that is used and in northern England it is combined with dandelion root to make a tonic beer which also purifies the blood. The roots are lifted in August, a year after the seed is sown and they may extend for up to 2 ft (60 cm). The roots are dried and then cut into small pieces and boiled. At home, 1 oz (28 g) of root is boiled in 2 pt (1 litre) of water and after straining, take a wineglassful three times daily. It is made more palatable and effective if combined with sarsaparilla and is the best of all nature's cures for eczema. It is also demulcent and will soothe stomach disorders, likewise the leaves, an infusion of which when applied externally, will remove skin blemishes and a poultice made from the leaves will heal boils and the swellings of rheumatic joints. The plant may also be used as a vegetable, the young shoots being removed when about 8 in (20 cm) high and simmered in a little moisture until tender. Serve with melted butter like asparagus, to accompany meats. Like asparagus, burdock acts on the kidneys and will rid the bladder of impurities.

Seed is sown in drills made 20 in (50 cm) apart, thinning to 8 in (20 cm) in the rows. Of extreme hardiness, the plant grows well and is prolific in northern England.

CARAWAY (*Carum carvi*) S   A biennial growing about 2 ft (60 cm) tall, it is found over the whole of the northern hemisphere and in Britain but mostly in Essex and East Anglia where the seed will ripen in a year of above average sunshine. It has a parsnip-like root and bi-pinnate leaves cut into linear lobes, while the fruit (seed) is boat-shaped hence its name which is derived from the Celtic *caroh* (a ship). The roots, seeds and leaves possess a peculiar aromatic smell, pleasing to some but unpleasant to others. The essential oil is mixed with that of lavender and used in the manufacture of cheaper toilet soaps and is used to flavour the liqueur, Kummel. In Shakespeare's time, and today in Ireland, the seed is used to flavour bread and cakes and to serve with apples, a dish always being on the table when apples are served as dessert. To make a water to relieve indigestion, infuse 1 oz (28 g) of seed in 1 pt (570 ml) of hot water and take a dessertspoonful when necessary. It is warming and comforting to the stomach.

Parkinson said that the roots boiled in water and served with white sauce to accompany fish or meat 'warm and comfort a cold, weak stomach'. After harvesting the seed, the roots can be used during winter.

Seed is sown in drills made 18 in (45 cm) apart in July, thinning to 10 in (25 cm) apart in the rows in spring. The plants will need supporting for the seeds to ripen properly.

CENTAURY (*Centaurium erythraea*)   An annual growing about 8 in (20 cm) tall, it was named in honour of the centaur, Chiron, and owing to its bitterness was known as 'gall of the earth'. Usually found growing in limestone soil, it forms a rosette of pointed leaves from which arise unstalked pink flowers which open only in sunlight and close up at noon.

The plant has many medicinal uses. The fresh or dried leaves, together with those of St John's wort, infused in boiling water, will strengthen the bladder and prevent bed-wetting by children and old people while an infusion of the flowering tops (a handful to 1 pt (570 ml) of hot water) will relieve indigestion if taken after a meal, a wineglassful at a time.

Women would wash their face in centaury water as it would take away skin blemishes and the juice of the leaves applied to sores and abrasions would heal them quickly.

Sow the seed in spring, in small groups at the front of a border or in drills made 6 in (15 cm) apart, thinning to 4 in (10 cm) apart, thinning to 4 in (10 cm) in the rows. It blooms June-August.

CHERVIL (*Chaerophyllum cerifolium*)   An annual or biennial, growing 16 in (40 cm) tall, its hollow stems covered in silky hairs. Its three-pinnate leaves emit an aniseed smell when handled. The roots also have a similar scent and were candied like eringoes (the root of the sea-holly) to enjoy as sweetmeats but are poisonous unless first boiled. The foliage however, is pleasantly sweet when used in salads and from the leaves, a delicious sauce to serve with fish is made.

For a continuous supply, make a sowing about 1 August, in drills made 12 in (30 cm) apart or to the front of a border and cover with cloches during winter. Make another sowing in April and again in June and this will provide fresh young leaves from early summer until the end of autumn. Begin using the leaves as soon as they form as the more they are cut, the bushier and more prolific does the plant become.

CLARY (*Salvia horminoides*) A hairy biennial of considerable beauty growing about 2 ft (60 cm) tall with deeply toothed dark green leaves, serrated at the edges. The sage-like flowers are violet-blue with two white marks on the lower lip and appear from June until September. It grows wild in damp meadows, usually south of the Thames but may be a garden escape and requires a soil containing plenty of humus. Its name is a corruption of 'clear eyes' for an infusion of the leaves will relieve tired and inflamed eyes. The leaves have a refreshing pineapple scent, and in France a wine noted for its narcotic qualities is made from them, while the French also use the essential oil in perfumery. The leaves are also included, when dry, in *pot pourris* and one or two in an omelette, sprinkled with lemon juice will give it a delicious flavour.

Clary is propagated by seed sown in July in shallow drills. Set out the young plants 18 in (45 cm) apart towards the front of the flower border where it is completely at home, with borage and marigolds.

CORIANDER (*Coriandrum sativum*) S   An annual to be found naturalised in parts of Essex and East Anglia, it may have come with the Romans for it is native of the Levant and northern Africa. Pliny said that the best seed came from Egypt as it does to this day. The seed is large, round and pale yellow and when ripe has the pleasing smell of oranges. When unripe, it smells, as does the whole plant, unpleasantly of bugs and takes its name from the Greek *koros* (a bug). Growing about 10 in (25 cm) tall it has dark green bi-pinnate leaves, divided into deeply cut segments.

In Britain it will ripen its seeds only in a summer of above average sunshine and is grown in East Anglia, Essex and Kent. Coriander water to relieve flatulence is made by pouring 1 pt (570 ml) of boiling water on a teaspoonful of seed and a tablespoonful is taken when needed. The seed is included in curry powders and a few added to a blancmange will impart a pleasant orange taste. The dried leaves and seeds are used to flavour soups and broths but do not use them when fresh.

To ripen its seed, choose an open situation and sow early April, in drills made 6 in (15 cm) apart, thinning to the same distance in the rows. The seeds will ripen better if the plants are grown in poor soil.

CORNFLOWER (*Centaurea cyanus*)   An annual or biennial, it is a rare native plant of cornfields, its deep blue flowers having blue anthers. It grows 16 in (40 cm) tall, with narrow slightly toothed leaves which, infused in hot water, make an effective mouth wash, while the juice rubbed on to cuts 'quickly solder up the lips of them'. In Germany and other northern European countries, the leaves are put into ale as they are effective in cases of jaundice. Painters of old would pound the blue flowers with a little alum which they incorporated into their oils.

A handsome plant for the border, the flowers are borne solitary during July and August and are most attractive when growing near grey-leaved plants. Seed is sown in August or in April in small groups, thinning the plants to 6 in (15 cm) apart.

Cornflower

CUMIN (*Cumynum cyminum*) S A slender annual at one time cultivated in East Anglia for its seed which now comes from Egypt, northern Africa and Malta for it requires plenty of sunshine to ripen. The plant grows about 18 in (45 cm) tall with fern-like leaves and bears tiny white flowers followed by large elongated seeds. Mentioned in Isaiah, the seeds are still used in the East to flavour bread and cakes but in the west are almost entirely used in pickles and chutneys and in curry powders. 4 oz (110 g) of the seed, together with 4 oz (110 g) of coriander, $\frac{1}{2}$ oz (14 g) of allspice and 4 oz (110 g) of turmeric, ground in a mortar and kept in a screw-top jar will provide an excellent curry powder to use as required. The water made by pouring 1 pt (570 ml) on to a teaspoonful of seed will relieve flatulence and indigestion if a dessertspoonful is taken when necessary.

It will ripen its seed, in a good summer in East Anglia, Essex and Kent. Seed is sown in spring in drills made 10 in (25 cm) apart, thinning the plants to 8 in (20 cm) in the rows.

DILL (*Anethum graveolens*) S   It may have come with the Romans and grew wild in England in Saxon times for it is mentioned in several of the old leech books. Indeed, it takes its name from the Saxon, *dilla* (to lull) for women would rub dill water on to the breasts when feeding a child and it would lull the baby to sleep. It is a carminative and a tablespoonful of dill water taken at bedtime will calm the nerves and bring about sound sleep.

Dill is an annual growing just over 3 ft (1 m) tall with finely cut foliage which has a spicy taste which it imparts to garden peas and new potatoes if a few leaves are boiled with them. A sauce is made from the leaves to serve with fish and the seeds are used in pickles and to make dill vinegar. This is made by boiling 2 pt (1 litre) of malt vinegar and $\frac{1}{4}$ oz (7 g) of dill seeds. Strain and allow to cool before bottling.

Excellent for relieving indigestion and stomach pains, and as a gripe-water for children, pour 1 pt (570 ml) of boiling water on to a teaspoonful of seeds and take a dessert spoonful when necessary.

Seed is sown in spring in drills made 12 in (30 cm) apart and an open situation is necessary for the seeds to ripen. Thin to 10 in (25 cm) apart in the rows.

EYEBRIGHT (*Euphrasia officinalis*)   An annual growing only 4 in (10 cm) tall with small deeply cut leaves and bearing tiny lilac flowers veined with purple which appear from June until September. It takes its name from the Greek, *euphrasono* (I clear) in allusion to is ability to clear the eyes of cataract. Whether or not this is so is hard to determine but if the plant is infused in hot milk and when lukewarm, it is used to bathe the eyes at bedtime, it will by morning, have given them a brilliance that no other preparation is able to do. For this reason, herbal beauty shops are enjoying a considerable demand for eyebright lotion.

Common on waste ground, it grows readily from seed sown in drills in spring and made 6 in (15 cm) apart. Cut off the plants near soil level, when required to make up an eye lotion. An infusion

125

will also stop running eyes caused by hay fever or cold winds.

MARIGOLD (*Calandula officinalis*) See the chapter on herbs in the kitchen garden.

MULLEIN (*Verbaseum thapsus*) See the chapter on herbs in the flower border.

MUSTARD, Black (*Brassica nigra*) S An annual which is grown commercially in Lincolnshire and East Anglia to supply large quantities of the seed to make the condiment. Since Tudor times it has been a desirable accompaniment for beef and steak, ever since the plant was first grown near Tewkesbury in Shakespeare's day. Parkinson suggested grinding the seeds between stones (known as 'queens') and adding a little vinegar to the flour 'to make a sauce both for fish and flesh' and in this way mustard powder or flour has been used ever since. Grilled herrings and mustard sauce is much enjoyed on the north eastern coast of England and Scotland and is to be recommended.

In Dijon, France, fine mustard has been made since the thirteenth century, using tarragon vinegar, anchovies and capers. In 1382, Philip the Bold granted armorial bearings to the town in recognition of its mustard making.

Mustard is both antiseptic and a deodoriser and a little flour in a utensil swilled out with 1 pt (570 ml) of hot water will remove any unpleasant smell or taste. It will do the same for the hands if washed in it.

If the feet are placed in a bowl of mustard and hot water at bedtime, it will bring out a head cold better than anything and will warm the body if chilled outdoors in cold weather.

Black mustard flour is readily available, and the plant is not grown in the garden.

For 'mustard and cress,' white mustard is grown, sowing it on damp cloth or in boxes or pots of soil all the year round. In a winter temperature of 48° F (8° C) it will be ready to cut within three weeks. To have the two ready together, sow the cress four to five days earlier and include them in salads and in sandwiches. White mustard has a pleasant bitterness.

PARSLEY PIERT (*Sison amomum*) A slender glabrous biennial of branching habit with bi-pinnate leaves which when pressed, release the unpleasant smell of ammonia. Widespread by the wayside especially in calcareous soils, it is the best of all nature's cures for breaking stone in the kidneys for which reason it has always been known as 'breakstone'. Culpeper said that 1 drachm of the dried and powdered leaf taken in a wineglassful of white wine would 'bring away gravel without pain'; or infuse a handful of fresh leaves in 1 pt (570 ml) of boiling water and, when cool, take a wineglassful twice daily.

Grow it in the vegetable garden rather than in the border for it all too readily seeds itself. Sow it in July, in drills 12 in (30 cm) apart and thin to 6 in (15 cm) in the rows. Towards the end of summer, remove the remaining leaves and dry them in a warm, airy room, then rub down and store in glass jars to use as required.

SHEPHERD'S PURSE (*Capsella bursa-pastoris*)   Found in cornfields and by the roadside everywhere, it is an annual growing only 4 in (10 cm) tall, the root leaves forming a rosette, while the small white flowers are borne in terminal racemes the whole year round except in the coldest weather. It was named 'purse' perhaps for its small flattened seed pods which resemble a purse or because it was a cheap remedy for various ailments.

An infusion of the leaves (or seeds) will stay internal bleeding and in the USA it is taken for dropsy, for which infuse a small handful of leaves in 1 pt (570 ml) of hot water and take a wineglassful twice daily. The juice of the leaves rubbed on to bruises will quickly heal them, likewise a handful of leaves in a warm bath. It is a crucifer and the leaves contain iron, sulphur and other mineral salts like those of watercress and Lady's Smock and were included with boiled cabbage in spring to improve the health. But it is to arrest internal bleeding that the plant is of such importance.

It is a common plant of the countryside but grows quickly from seed sown in spring at the front of a border or in drills made 6 in (15 cm) apart.

SOWTHISTLE (*Sonchus oleraceous*)   An annual growing 3–4 ft (1 m) tall, with hollow stems and toothed leaves covered in soft prickles. It is widespread on waste ground everywhere. Its name is a corruption of two Anglo-Saxon words 'surve-distel' (sprout-thistle) for the young sprouting shoots in early summer were boiled to serve with meat or fish when vegetables were scarce. The young shoots are delicious steamed in butter and served with poached eggs on buttered toast. Countrywomen would wash their face in the juice mixed with a little warm water or use the water in which the shoots were boiled for it is an effective skin rejuvenator and removes unsightly blemishes. Only when the plants are old, at the end of summer, are they full of juice.

As it tends to seed readily and become a nuisance in the border, sow it in an out-of-the-way corner, in drills 10 in (25 cm) apart and thin to the same distance in the rows. Do this by using the young shoots in early summer.

SWEET BASIL (*Ocimum basilicum*)   In its native India it is a perennial but owing to its inability to survive an English winter it is treated here as a half-hardy annual, the seed being sown in drills about 1 May; or in pots in which the plants are grown on in a sunny window when they will retain their leaves for almost twelve months. It was grown in this way in Tudor times when Tusser said that

> Fine basil desireth it may be her lot,
> To grow as the gillyflower, trim in a pot.

In the East it is usually grown in this way for the plant is held sacred to the gods Krishna and Vishnu and when growing indoors it is worshipped by the entire household.

Sweet basil is a much-branched plant growing about 16 in (40 cm) tall and when in pots should be supported by thin canes. It has dark green ovate lance-shaped leaves which when pressed, release the most delicious scent of all herbs, being warm and spicy, almost clove-like. There is a bronze leaf variety, Dark Opal which makes a striking pot plant.

Sweet basil is the best of all herbs to accompany tomato dishes, whether cooked or served raw in salads. 'Basil,' said Evelyn 'imparts a grateful flavour to salads' and it can be included with tomatoes in omelettes and dried or fresh, used to flavour soups and stews while a delicious sauce to accompany fish is made from the fresh leaves.

Basil 'tea' helps the digestion and is warming and soothing to the stomach while the dried leaves taken as snuff, will clear a stuffed up nose due to a head cold.

If planting outdoors, provide a soil containing some humus and an open, sunny situation. Do not plant out until early May in the south; the month end in the north and then only after hardening the plants. Set them about 10 in (25 cm) apart, the dwarf Bush basil, 0. minimum 6 in (15 cm) apart. Early autumn, cut the plants down at soil level and string up to dry in any airy room, like sage.

Annual and biennial herbs (S) = seeds

Herb	Botanical name	When available	Use
Alkanet	*Anchusa officinalis*	Summer	Restorative and astringent
Anise (S)	*Pimpinella anisum*	All year	Coughs and flatulence
Borage	*Borago officinalis*	Summer	In drinks
Burdock	*Arctium lappa*	Summer	Blood purifier
Caraway (S)	*Carum carvi*	All year	Flavouring
Centaury	*Centaurium erythraea*	Summer	Strengthens the bladder
Coriander (S)	*Coriandrum sativum*	All year	Flatulence and for flavouring
Cornflower	*Centaurea cyanus*	Summer	Mouth wash
Cumin (S)	*Cumynum cyminum*	All year	In curry powders
Dill (S)	*Anethum graveolens*	All year	Carminative
Eyebright	*Euphrasia officinalis*	Summer	For eyes
Marigold	*Calendula officinalis*	All year	In broths and for complexion
Mustard, Black (S)	*Brassica nigra*	All year	Condiment
Parsley Piert	*Sison amomum*	Summer	For the kidneys

Herbs	Botanical name	When available	Use
Shepherd's Purse	*Capsella bursa-pastoris*	Summer	Stay bleeding
Sowthistle	*Sonchus oleraceous*	Summer	Vegetable
Sweet basil	*Ocimum basilicum*	Summer	To accompany fish and tomato dishes

Coltsfoot

Medicinal Herbs and their Uses

There are several herbs that are grown almost entirely for their medicinal uses and though perennial are best grown in a part of the garden to themselves rather than in the border. Several are of climbing or semi-climbing habit and are difficult to site except by growing them against a trellis which may be used to divide the medicinal plants from those which have culinary value. A number of the medicinal herbs have a deep penetrating rootstock which makes them difficult to eradicate should they become too prolific. Amongst these are the coltsfoot, horehound and liquorice. But they are amongst the most useful of plants and should not be omitted from the garden though most are widely distributed about the countryside and are there for the taking.

Herbs of medicinal value

COLTSFOOT (*Tussilago farfara*)   A low-growing perennial common on waste ground everywhere, it has large heart-shaped leaves and drooping yellow flowers borne on leafless stems. One of the first plants to bloom, it opens in the February sunshine but it is an obnoxious weed in gardens and should be confined to an out-of-the-way corner where seed is sown in April, in drills 8 in (20 cm) apart, thinning to 10 in (25 cm) in the rows. The dried and ground leaves, together with those of chamomile and wood betony, make up a pleasant herbal smoking mixture which will relieve asthma or a hard cough. Sticks of coltsfoot rock, taken for a cough or tight chest were one of the delicacies of childhood days. The plant takes its name from *tussis ago* (I drive away a cough). To relieve bronchitis, a handful of leaves simmered in 2 pt (1 litre) of water for thirty minutes and sweetened with a little honey, should be taken in small amounts every two hours. The plant contains tannin and the same infusion, when warm, can be used as a gargle to ease a sore throat.

COMFREY (*Symphytum officinale*) A hairy perennial growing about 2 ft (60 cm) tall with branched leafy stems and elliptical leaves. The pink and blue flowers are borne in elliptical clusters in July and August. Widespread in ditches, it requires a moist soil containing humus. It is readily raised from seed sown in a frame or under cloches in spring, transplanting the seedlings in July 20 in (50 cm) apart to permanent quarters. As an external healer it has no equal and the whole plant beaten to a pulp and bound over a cut or sore will quickly heal it; or it may be used as an ointment. Boil 1 lb (450 g) of the plant in ½ lb (225 g) of lard, strain and pour into screw-top jars before it is cool and use when necessary. Comfrey oil helps sprains, bruises and rheumatic joints if gently massaged into the skin – affected parts.

GROUND IVY (*Nepeta glechoma*) A semi-trailing perennial of the catmint family, releasing the familiar pungent minty smell when the leaves are pressed. With its small heart-shaped leaves, sage-green in colour and marked with white and cream and its small purple-blue flowers borne from April until August, it is one of the most interesting plants of the herb garden. It is attractive in a hanging basket or when trailing down from a window box and it will retain its leaves all the year. Like the periwinkle, it will grow in semi-shade and is present in open woodlands and hedgerows. Before the use of hops, it grew in every ale-house garden for it clarified ale, hence it name ale-hoof though its botanical name is from Nepet, in Tuscany where it abounds and glechon, mint. From it, a tonic drink was made and sold in ale-houses as 'gill tea', gill-by-the-ground being one of the plant's country names. Taken hot, it will relieve a hard cough if sweetened with honey and it is a blood purifier. It figures in the foot-baths of the French herbal practitioner, Mons. Maurice Messegué for the relief of asthma and, for the same purpose, the dried and powdered leaves are used with those of chamomile and betony, to take as snuff and to use in a smoking mixture.

The plant sends out long stems which root at the leaf nodes when in contact with the soil and these can be detached and replanted in small pots or the open ground. It is happy in semi-shade and in ordinary soil.

HOP (*Humulus lupulus*) A perennial which will climb to 16 ft (5 m) and in the garden is grown against a trellis. It takes its name from the Anglo-Saxon, *hoppan* (to climb). The plant first came to be used for brewing early in the seventeenth century. Before that, ale was made from malt and clarified with ground ivy. The plant is present in open woodlands and hedgerows in southern England but is rare elsewhere in Britain. The three to five lobed leaves are coarsely serrated, the male flowers being borne in a catkin-like inflorescence, the females in the axils of the bracts as a cylindrical spike. The bracteoles bear glandular hairs which yield the golden dust, lupulin now an important ingredient of the brewing industry.

The narcotic effects of hops are well known and to induce deep sleep, a pillow stuffed with dry hops will be more effective than anything as well as being pleasantly fragrant. The drier the hops become the more scented will they be and they may be used to fill muslin bags, together with dried woodruff and agrimony, to place in a pillow or beneath a pillow case. If properly dried, they will retain their fragrance for several years.

From a handful of hops, a pleasant tonic drink is made. Pour $\frac{1}{2}$ pt (275 ml) of boiling water on to a handful of hops (or leaves), strain and take a wineglassful twice daily, preferably from the refrigerator.

To raise plants to cover a trellis, seed is sown in a frame in spring, the young plants being set out 20 in (50 cm) apart when large enough to handle. Provide the plants with some humus in the soil and keep well watered. The foliage turns brown in autumn as the plant dies back but will come again in spring.

HOREHOUND (*Marrubium vulgare*)   A perennial growing about 16 in (40 cm) tall, its square stems covered in woolly down like hoar frost and with deeply furrowed bluntly-toothed leaves. The white flowers are borne in whorls throughout summer and are visited by bees. Widespread by the wayside, especially in calcareous soils in England but rare elsewhere in Britain, it takes its name from the Hebrew, *marrob* (a bitter juice) and before the introduction of hops, a tonic beer was brewed from the leaves. A 'tea' which is a tonic and appetiser, is made by pouring 1 pt (570 ml) of hot water over a handful of leaves. Strain when cool and take a wineglassful twice daily, an hour before lunch and at supper time. When warmed by the sun, the leaves emit a pleasing musky perfume and although they lose this in winter, they remain green all the year.

With coltsfoot, syrup of horehound is one of the best of all remedies for a cough. It is made by boiling 1 lb (450 g) of leaves with 2 pt (1 litre) of water, then strain and re-heat the liquid, adding ½ lb (225 g) of sugar. When the sugar has melted, allow to cool and pour into bottles, using a teaspoonful when a winter cough is troublesome.

To candy horehound, boil 1 lb (450 g) of leaves with 2 lb (900 g) of sugar. Strain and re-heat, pour into a shallow dish and allow to cool. Then cut the candy into 1 in (2·5 cm) squares and keep in a tightly closed tin. Take a piece for a hard cough or tight chest.

Seed is sown in spring in shallow drills made 12 in (30 cm) apart, thinning to 8 in (20 cm) apart in the rows. The plants can also be propagated by root division in March and are attractive in the border with their silvery-green stems. It requires a well drained soil and an open situation.

HOUSELEEK (*Sempervivum tectorum*)   The word 'Leek' is derived from the Anglo-Saxon *leac* which means a plant growing on a roof and this is where it is usually to be found, on old buildings growing from the cracks of Collyweston stone slates, protecting the house against thunder and lightning or so it was believed that it would do. A fleshy perennial, it forms a rosette of pointed leaves, the juice of which Parkinson said 'taketh away corns from the feet';

of great importance at a time when the feet were used to do most jobs on the land. The leaves contain an astringent juice which is present also in malic acid of apples and two drops in a dessert-spoonful of water will help in cases of diarrhoea and dysentery. The juice, rubbed on burns, will take away the inflammation and the same when used as an ointment. The plant retains its leaves so can be used all the year.

It is propagated from seed sown in pots or boxes in a frame or sunny window and the plants can be grown on in pots in which they can spend their whole life which may be fifty years or more. Propagation is also by offsets which form around the plant and there are many attractive species and varieties to add to a collection. Provide the plants with a porous compost, containing sand and shingle and in winter, give them very little moisture. They add interest to an old wall or outhouse roof which is covered with stone slates.

LESSER CELANDINE (*Ranunculus ficaria*) A perennial growing in damp woodlands and on low-lying ground in most parts of the British Isles. It is one of the first of the spring flowers to bloom, opening it golden-yellow buttercup-like flowers, held on 4 in (10 cm) long stems, in March. It has pretty dark-green cordate leaves which when boiled in lard and strained and allowed to cool, will give relief to the most stubborn piles, hence to the countryman it was known as pilewort. The leaves are astringent and used in beauty treatments. Immerse a handful in 1 pt (570 ml) of boiling water, strain and when cool, apply to the face with lint. It will close the pores, tighten the skin and remove wrinkles.

Seed is sown in spring in pots and boxes and the seedlings set out 6 in (15 cm) apart at the front of a border or in small beds. Dig some humus into the soil before planting.

LESSER PERIWINKLE (*Vinca minor*) An almost prostrate perennial with wiry stems which can be used in a hanging basket or planted to the front of a border. Like ground ivy, it is of semi-trailing habit and the stems root at the leaf nodes when in contact with the soil, this being the best method of propagation. The stems are detached and the rooted pieces planted into small pots or in

135

the open ground. This is done in early autumn so that the plants are re-established before winter.

Common throughout England in semi-shaded woodlands and hedgerows, it is a valuable ground-cover plant which grows well in shade. It is also extremely hardy and can be planted in a northerly aspect and in a cold exposed garden. It is also evergreen and grows well in any type of soil so that in Germany it is taken as the emblem of immortality. Like rosemary in other countries, it was used at funerals and weddings, the long string-like stems being woven into chaplets to wear at both occasions.

The plant has much the same medicinal qualities as the lesser celandine. If the bruised leaves are boiled with lard, the ointment will heal bleeding piles and tincture made from the leaves and spirits of wine will check internal haemorrhage if two drops are taken in a dessertspoonful of water twice daily. A decoction made from a handful of the leaves and a pint of boiling water makes a capital gargle to ease a sore throat if used when warm.

The plant has glossy dark green leaves and bears its violet-blue flowers from mid-March right through summer.

LIQUORICE (*Glycyrrhiza glabra*) Native of southern Europe, northern Africa and sub-tropical Asia, it is a perennial which increases by its underground rootstock and it grows 3–4 ft (1 m) tall, with pinnate leaves. It has been cultivated in England, in the Pontefract district of Yorkshire, since Tudor times or earlier, to supply the sweet makers and chemists, to make cough mixtures and laxatives while the juice obtained from the roots, adds thickness, sweetness and the rich brown colour to stout, to which it imparts its many health-giving qualities.

It is the roots that are used for the extraction of the juice, after drying. The dried roots have for hundreds of years, been imported into Britain from Spain, hence liquorice sticks came to be called Spanish juice. Only when the extract is obtained from the dried roots is it clear and bright. Together with elecampane and the distilled water of aniseed and fennel, it makes a nourishing beer and from the juice, mixed with a little linseed, a 'tea' is made which acts as a tonic and gentle laxative.

As the roots will penetrate to a depth of 3–4 ft (1 m), the ground must be well prepared and a light well-drained soil is essential, so too is clean ground for the plants are left to grow for at least three years before the roots are large enough to use. To plant, cut the roots into pieces 3–4 in (7·5–10 cm) long, each with two 'buds', rather like rhubarb thongs, and set them in October 12 in (30 cm) apart and just below the surface of the soil. This is also the time of year to lift them, at the same time replanting the smaller roots to maintain a supply.

The roots are lifted with care and it is necessary to go well down to prevent the lower portions from breaking off. Lift when the soil is as dry as possible and leave in the sun for several hours. Then knock off the soil and place on a bench in a warm airy room to complete the drying which will take several weeks.

To extract the juice, place the dried roots in a brass pan (as used for making jam) and immerse them in cold water for twenty-four hours, using 3 fl oz (75 ml) of water to every 1 oz (28 g) of root. Then bring to the boil and maintain this until a thick consistency is obtained. Strain through flannel or muslin into earthenware jars.

LUNGWORT (*Pulmonaria officinalis*)   An attractive perennial growing 10 in (25 cm) tall, its long-stemmed oval leaves terminating to a point and being spotted with white, as the lungs were thought to look like and so the plant is a good example of the *Doctrine of Signatures*. The flowers with their funnel-shaped corolla resemble those of the cowslip but are a mixture of blue and rose. They appear at the same time as the cowslip but are found in woodlands and hedgerows of southern England. The plant was known as 'soldiers and sailors' for the red colouring denotes the red tunics worn by our army at Waterloo and the blue represents sailor's tunics at Trafalgar.

The leaves boiled in a little milk were once drunk for lung diseases and they were used as a poultice for lung congestion. It is a plant for a border or for semi-shade and ordinary well drained soil is suitable. Propagation is by root division in spring, planting the offsets about 9 in (22 cm) apart; or from seed sown in pots or boxes in spring.

NETTLE (*Urtica dioica*)   A perennial and so common about the

137

countryside, on wasteland and in farmyards that it is not grown in gardens, yet it is one of nature's finest cures for blood pressure and the young leaves in spring make a nourishing dish if cooked (steamed) in a little butter and served with meats. For this purpose, nettle tops were sold in the streets of London. Boiled nettles are fed to young turkeys during the difficult rearing stage with excellent results and from the boiled tops a poultice can be made (the tops being placed in a large muslin bag), that John Wesley said was the best of all cures for sciatica. It should be applied to the buttocks as warm as possible after draining away surplus moisture.

To reduce blood pressure, nettle 'tea' has no equal. Dry the young leaves, place a handful in a jug and add 1 pt (570 ml) of boiling water. When cool, strain and add a little lemon juice and drink a wineglassful twice daily. It is more palatable if used straight from the refrigerator. It will also purify the blood, improve the complexion, and relieve asthmatic attacks. For this too, and to relieve bronchitis, countrymen would dry and burn the leaves in winter over hot embers, to fill the room with the pungent smell.

The plant takes its name from the Anglo-Saxon *needl* (a needle) in reference to its stinging needle-like hairs at the base of which is a tiny globule of formic acid which is released into the skin when in contact, causing a sharp pain followed by irritation and

Stinging Nettle

soreness. To cure nettle stings quickly, rub the affected part with a dock leaf or with mint.

The nettle is an unbranched perennial growing 2 ft (60 cm) tall with toothed leaves from the axils of which are borne tiny greenish-white flowers. It is distinguished from the Dead nettle (which has no sting) for the latter has a square stem and is a labiate with white flowers borne in whorls which are much visited by bees for the large amount of honey secreted.

PLANTAIN (*Plantago major*) It is the Greater plantain, a low-growing perennial with long spoon-shaped leaves and minute green flowers borne in long spikes at the end of leafless stems. It was known as waybroad for it is always found by the wayside. Shakespeare alludes to its use in healing bruises and its leaves were used, together with southernwood, elder buds and blackcurrant leaves, to make a renowned Devonshire healing ointment or salve. Culpeper said that a decoction of the leaves was healing for mouth sores if used as a mouth wash and the crushed leaves and stems give relief to piles. It had so many uses, the plant was taken to America by the New England settlers.

If required in the garden, plants can be lifted from wasteland and replanted in small groups with other medicinal plants.

RAGWORT (*Senecio jacobea*) A perennial growing 3 ft (90 cm) tall, and widespread on chalkland in north eastern England. It has deeply lobed leaves and bears yellow flowers in flat terminal clusters all summer. Since earliest times it has been used to heal cuts and wounds, also skin sores, the stems and leaves being crushed and boiled with fresh lard to make into an ointment. Also, a poultice made from the plant and applied hot, will do much to relieve rheumatic pains and sprains.

A garden weed, it readily seeds itself and is best grown with other herbs of similar qualities, sowing the seed in spring in drills made 12 in (30 cm) apart and thinning to 6 in (15 cm) in the rows. It is attractive when in seed, the grey seed pappus resembling silver hair, hence its name of Old Man.

WHITE BRIONY (*Bryonia dioica*) A perennial, common in hedge-rows in southern England and East Anglia and climbing by means of tendrils. It has large five-lobed leaves and bears greenish flowers through summer which are followed by poisonous red berries. It takes its name from the Greek *bruein*, (to shoot up rapidly). It is the root that is used and in two to three years it will grow as thick as a man's arm. Lint saturated in a decoction of the root and placed over bruises will quickly remove soreness and discolouration. Four drops of the tincture of the roots taken in a little water every four hours will give relief to rheumatic pains. Countrymen have found that a nourishing drink is obtained from the roots known as 'hop bitters'.

The best way of growing it in the garden is to plant the seeds at the base of a hedge so that the plant will pull itself up through the hedge and once planted, it will seed itself.

WOOD BETONY (*Stachys betonica*)   A hairy perennial growing about 20 in (50 cm) tall with a slender stem and oblong deeply crenate leaves. The reddish purple flowers are borne in a terminal spike all summer and are much visited by bees. The plant is present in open woodlands and of it, Parkinson said, 'the aromatic leaves by their sweet and spicy taste are comfortable both in meat and medicine'. Gerard said that the young leaves in a salad were 'good for the appetite' but it is for nervous headaches that the plant has always been held in most esteem. The dried and powdered leaves were included in medicated snuffs to relieve head pains and the fresh leaves, placed on the forehead and temples and held in place with damp cold flannel will quickly remove the most stubborn headache. From the fresh leaves too, a 'tea' is made (a handful to 1 pt (570 ml) of water) which if taken a wineglassful at bedtime, will quickly relieve head pains caused by nervous tension.

Wood betony is a handsome plant for the border growing 2 ft (60 cm) tall and being long in bloom, when the richly coloured flowers are enhanced by the dark green leaves. The plant will grow well in semi-shade but requires a light well drained soil to be long living. It is however, readily raised from seed sown in pots or boxes in spring and transplanting the young plants 16 in (40 cm) apart in July. They will then be nicely established before winter.

WOODRUFF (*Asperula odorata*)   An almost prostrate perennial with four angled stems, growing about 8 in (20 cm) tall, the lanceolate leaves produced in whorls of six to nine. Widespread in the British Isles in open woodlands, hedgerows and on mountainous slopes, usually of limestone formations, the plant is scentless as it grows, but when dry emits the refreshing scent of newly mown hay for it is rich in coumarin. This is also present in the sweet vernal grass of meadows, and the drier the plant becomes, the more powerful is its scent. Its country name tells us that it is a woodland plant and that its leaves form a ruff, like the Tudors wore around the neck, from the Anglo-Saxon *rofe* (a wheel).

Remaining fragrant for many months when dry, cottagers would hang up the plant when it would keep the rooms cool in summer and pleasantly scented. In Georgian times, gentlemen would detach a whorl of leaves by cutting it from the stem and when dry, would place it in the back of a pocket watch, to inhale when in a stuffy atmosphere. The dried plant was put into muslin bags to place amongst clothes and linen to impart its fragrance and as a moth deterrent. Pillows and mattresses were stuffed with it (together with dried hops) and when laid upon, would release a pleasing and sleep inducing fragrance.

A tonic drink with blood purifying properties was made by immersing a handful of plants in 1 pt (570 ml) of boiling water, straining and taking a wineglassful daily throughout summer. Plants are readily raised from seed sown in spring in shallow drills and thinned to 6 in (15 cm) apart.

Woodruff is shade loving and should be grown with other medicinal herbs enjoying similar conditions.

VALERIAN (*Valeriana officinalis*) A perennial growing 2–3 ft (60–90 cm) tall, it has dark green pinnate leaves and in July and August bears numerous pale pink flowers in a terminal cyme. Found in moist woodlands and hedgerows, mostly in England and Wales and usually in a limestone soil, it takes its name from the Latin *valeo* (to be well) because of its many healing qualities. It is the roots that are used and although an attractive border plant, it is usually confined to a part of the garden where it can be lifted without disturbing other plants.

Still listed in the British *Pharmacopaeia*, the plants are lifted in autumn and dried, the offsets being replanted to maintain a stock. A decoction of 1 oz (28 g) of the roots in 1 pt (570 ml) of boiling water and taken a wineglassful twice daily, will calm the nerves and relieve a nervous headache. The leaves boiled in fresh lard and strained while hot, make a valuable healing ointment when allowed to cool and set. Pour into screw-top jars while still warm.

The plant is readily raised from seed sown in pots or boxes in spring and planted out in July 20 in (50 cm) apart; or it is propagated by root division in October or March. It requires a soil containing some humus, and for the roots to grow large provide the plants with moisture during dry weather.

Herbs with medicinal uses

Herb	Botanical name	When available	Use
Coltsfoot	*Tussilago farfara*	All year	For coughs and asthma
Comfrey	*Symphytum officinale*	All year	For external healing
Ground Ivy	*Nepeta glechoma*	All year	Blood purifier
Hop	*Humulus lupulus*	All year	Sleep inducing
Horehound	*Marrubium vulgare*	All year	For coughs; as a tonic
Houseleek	*Sempervivum tectorum*	All year	Astringent
Lesser Celandine	*Ranunculus ficaria*	Summer	For haemorrhoids
Lesser Periwinkle	*Vinca minor*	All year	For haemorrhoids
Liquorice	*Glycyrrhiza glabra*	All year	As tonic and for cough mixtures
Lungwort	*Pulmonaria officinalis*	All year	For lung ailments
Nettle	*Urtica dioica*	All year	For blood pressure
Plantain	*Plantago major*	Summer	Healing salve; astringent
Ragwort	*Senecio jacobea*	All year	Healing ointment

Herb	Botanical name	When available	Use
White Briony	*Bryonia dioica*	All year	Rheumatic pains
Wood Betony	*Stachys betonica*	All year	For head pains
Woodruff	*Asperula odorata*	All year	As a tonic
Valerian	*Valeriana officinalis*	All year	As carminative

Pot Pourri

Pot Pourris, Sweet Bags and Scented Waters

The uses of herbs in the kitchen and for simple remedies are without end. They are also of the greatest importance in providing the body with vitamins and mineral salts to maintain its health and there are also those sweetly scented herbs which satisfy the senses for as William Coles has written (1656), 'Herbs comfort the wearied brain with fragrant smells which yield a certain kind of nourishment', and Ralph Austen said that, 'sweet perfumes work immediately upon the spirits, for their refreshing, sweet and healthful ayres are special preservatives to health'. Few plants apart from the herbs of garden and countryside are able to give us so diverse a selection of delicious scents from their foliage which, when synthetic perfumes were unknown, gave of their fragrance in the homes of rich and poor alike. Every manor house and country cottage was redolent with its bowls of *pot pourri* which did much to hide the musty smell of rooms which had a stone floor and no damp course.

Leaves and their essential oils

In leaves, the essential oil is stored in cells, often as pellucid dots which in some leaves are visible to the naked eye as in bay and St John's Wort. Many plants with scented leaves contain substances not present in flowers and it is these which give them a refreshing pungent quality. Leaf scents are never cloying like the scents of certain flowers. They are also longer lasting, a well made *pot pourri* consisting mostly of leaves, retaining its fragrance for many years. As leaves dry, their fragrance intensifies. This is because of the evaporation of moisture from the leaves which causes the essential oil to remain in concentrated form and this is released when the leaf cells are broken when the leaf is pressed. With some herbs, the oil is stored deep down in the leaves and is not released without the leaf being subject to considerable pressure: in others it is stored just beneath the surface and so the fragrance is released with the slightest pressure as by a gentle breeze which wafts the scent of those herbs growing on Mediterranean islands far out to sea.

Of the many perfumes of plant leaves, borneol acetate with its powerful pine scent is present in rosemary as it is in pine needles and this gives rosemary its refreshing scent when placed in a bath. Eucalyptol, present in large amounts in the eucalyptus tree is also found in sage, thyme, wormwood, catmint and cotton lavender. It is also present in sweet bay but here it combines with the rose perfume (Geraniol) to give this plant a sweeter fragrance.

The development of the essential oil in a plant is highly complex. With lavender, the slightly scented linalol of the unripe bud combines with acetic acid to produce the bergamot-scented linalyl acetate of the fully open flower spike, though here it is the tiny bracts that are scented and not the actual flowers.

By the evaporation of moisture in sunlight, the linalyl acetate becomes geraniol, the principle substance of attar of roses and this gives the lavender its slight rose perfume which makes it one of the most popular of all plant scents.

Camphor too, is present in many herbs including those mentioned, also in yarrow, and citral is present in balm, southernwood and lemon-scented thyme as well as in lemon verbena which at one time was included in most *pot pourris*. Menthol, which gives the familiar minty smell to the mints is present in certain of the scented-leaf pelargoniums which can be grown in pots in a sunless window and their leaves used in *pot pourris* and sweet bags.

The combination of camphor and eucalyptol to be found in

145

wormwood, southernwood, rue and several other herbs, acts as a moth deterrent and the leaves of these plants have for long been used to place amongst clothes and linen. They are usually mixed with lavender and rosemary which have a sweeter perfume and which counteracts the more 'herby' scent of the others.

The delicious fruity scent which is rare in flowers is more often found in leaves. It is present in apple mint and pineapple sage, also in bergamot but here it is combined with camphor to give a slightly more 'herby' scent.

Herbs for *Pot Pourris*

When making up *pot pourris* or sweet bags, the blending of the various perfumes is important to the end product which should be both pleasing and refreshing. It is therefore important to blend together those herbs noted for their sweetness, such as lavender, rosemary and the petals of red roses, with those enjoyed for their 'herby' qualities which, on their own would be less attractive so that the more herbs that are grown, the wider will be the choice and the more pleasing the end product. Certain flowers such as clove-scented pinks and orange blossom (Philadelphus) can also be used but the greater part of a *pot pourri* should be made up of leaves.

The modern way of making a lasting *pot pourri* is to use one of the proprietary *pot pourri* makers concocted to a secret formula after years of experimenting and which will contain as many as thirty ingredients some of which may be difficult to find. But first, one must make up the *pot pourri* with those flowers and leaves of lasting fragrance, suitably dried and blended when the *pot pourri* maker will give it an enduring perfume but it cannot provide a fragrance which is not already there for it to act upon.

At one time, china *pot pourri* bowls or jars, attractively decorated were to be found in many homes. They were usually fitted with a lid or cover pierced with a number of holes which allowed the perfume to escape but kept the *pot pourri* free from dust and prevented it from being blown about the room whenever a window was opened. The containers, which today are antique items much sought after by collectors, will hold about 1 lb (450 g) of leaves and flower petals but when making up a *pot pourri*, any quantity can be made and a bowlful placed in every room. It will be much appreciated in a bedroom or sickroom.

There are both 'moist' and 'dry' *pot pourris*. A 'moist' *pot pourri* is made by using fresh ingredients, flowers and leaves which have not been dried. It can be made in an earthenware jar with a wide neck and which can often be found in stores and china shops, suitably decorated and fitted with a large cork. This is important where making a 'moist' *pot pourri* for it will long retain its perfume only if the cork or screw top is replaced after releasing the scent for a short time. The fragrance of a moist *pot pourri* will be extremely powerful and will fill a large room with its scent so that it is only necessary to release it for several minutes before the room is to be used, and then perhaps again later.

To make a 'moist' *pot pourri* to the recipe of Queen Henrietta Maria, wife of Charles I, begin by placing a 6 in (15 cm) layer of fresh red rose petals (those of Fragrant Cloud and Alec's Red are full of scent) in a jar and covering with a layer of salt about $\frac{1}{2}$ in (say 1 cm) deep. After a few days add other flower petals such as those of clove-scented pinks and orange blossom (Philadelphus). Include some lavender flowers rubbed from the stems and the leaves of bergamot, sweet marjoram and rosemary. A bay leaf or two is a necessary ingredient and some orange or lemon peel finely shredded. Cover with another layer of salt and leave for a few days, keeping the jar tightly closed. Then stir in a few dried or powdered cloves and replace the cork until the *pot pourri* is to be used. A jar decorated in modern style will be a pleasing ornament in any room and the perfume will be enjoyed by all who come in contact with it.

A 'dry' *pot pourri* need not be kept closed and will retain its fragrance in open bowls if correctly made. Both the flowers and leaves must be completely dry otherwise they will soon become mouldy and take on an unpleasant musty smell, like that of a damp room which is perhaps the very thing the *pot pourri* is being made to counteract. Both flowers and leaves should be harvested when dry, not until the morning dew has evaporated, and the flowers must be used when just fully open (not past their best) when they will be most fragrant. Leaves can be used at any age though will

147

have lost most of their essential oil if browned by frost or cold winds or have become too old.

A 'dry' *pot pourri* will give years of pleasure if made to this formula. To three parts of a basinful of rose petals dried slowly in an airy room, a cupful of dried rosemary, thyme and sweet marjoram and the dried and grated skin of an orange from which most of the pith has been removed, add a few powdered bay leaves, $\frac{1}{2}$ oz (14 g) of crushed cloves and a teaspoonful of allspice. Mix well together and add the *pot pourri* maker to give it a lasting fragrance, though the mixture will long retain its perfume if this is absent.

There may be those who would prefer a less sweet mixture and instead of using orange peel, use that of a lemon and in place of bay and sweet marjoram, use southernwood, balm and lemon thyme with a pinch of powdered nutmeg. It is a matter of taste and experiment. As flowers are more sweetly scented than leaves, use more of the latter where a less sweet mixture is required. A perfume may be increased or changed by using several of the less well known herbs, in particular the delicious pineapple-scented sage and the orange-scented thyme, *T. fragrantissimus*. The bergamot-scented leaves of the monarda can be used with them and cinnamon instead of nutmeg or cloves. Make up your *pot pourris* as summer advances, and beginning with the clove-scented pinks and red roses which appear in June. Orange blossom and lavender flowers come later but from early summer the leaves of most herbs are ready to use though their essential oil is most potent towards the end of summer, when much of the moisture from the leaves has evaporated.

Sweet bags and powders

Besides *pot pourris*, herbs and scented flowers can be made up into sweet bags to place amongst clothes and linen. Lavender has long been a favourite to place among handkerchiefs and under-clothes but it is not a moth deterrent and for this purpose it should be mixed with southernwood, wormwood or cotton lavender. The Tudors used the half opened buds of red roses to place among clothes. They were dried in an airy room and then sprinkled with powdered cinnamon or cloves which would trickle down between the petals. The buds were then placed into pretty muslin bags and tied up with ribbon to give as presents on birthdays.

Another method of making up a sweet bag is to take a basinful of red rose petals and the leaves of sweet marjoram, pineapple-scented sage and basil and to spread them out on trays in a warm airy room, an attic being suitable. Turn them daily until they are quite dry, then sprinkle them with cinnamon or cloves before making up into pretty bags.

To place beneath a pillow case, use instead the sleep-inducing herbs such as hops, chamomile, agrimony, woodruff, hyssop and marjoram, mixing several together of those that are available, after drying the leaves. Again, it a question of trial and error for some will act better with certain people, bringing about sleep quicker than with others.

Sweet powders were once made in every home and used much as we do modern talcum powders. One effective recipe is given by Mary Doggett in her *Book of Receipts* (1682) which is now in the Sloane Museum. Mary was the wife of the gentleman who in his will left a legacy for 'a coat and badge' to be contested yearly by Thames watermen and which some three centuries later, is still an important event of the August sporting calendar. Her recipe was to take a little ambergris or musk and to beat it with orange-flower water until it formed a thin paste. Into this was dipped whole cloves, one of which was put into a red or damask rose bud. When quite dry, the bud (and the clove) was beaten to a powder which was sprinkled about clothes and linen which would retain the powerful scent all the time it was on the bed.

The same lady also makes a number of suggestions for making scented powders using other ingredients, one of which is the violet scented orris powder. It is to dry rose petals with sweet marjoram and rosemary over a low fire until they are snuff dry, then to ground to a powder and mix in some orris. This is obtained from the root of the Florentine iris, symbol of the City of Florence which when dried and ground to a powder was and still is, used in many talcum powders. It was the favourite of Elizabeth I and powders were made for her from orris root, *Acorus calamus* (Sweet Flag), rose petals, cloves and storax which would retain their perfume for several years.

In his *Delights for Ladies*, the Elizabethan courtier, Sir Hugh Platt 'Knight of Lincoln's Inn' who had a famous garden nearby, tells how to perfume a room. This is to fill an earthenware jar with rose petals and the leaves of sweetly scented herbs and after heating them in a warm oven, to hang the jar by the side of 'a continual fire' when the ingredients will keep 'most delicate in scent' all winter. During Sir Hugh's time, rose petals and sweet scented leaves were sold from barrows in the streets of London at 6d a bushel, to make into *pot pourris*, scent bags and powders.

Sir Hugh also gives a reliable recipe for making a deliciously scented water. Obtain a large handful of lavender flowers which have been dried and mix with them some orris powder, a few crushed cloves and 4 oz (110 g) of benjamin. To the whole, add water to dilute and place in bowls in bedrooms to sprinkle on to clothes and over carpets and rush matting. Another of Sir Hugh's recipes to make a sweet water was to first make some rose water and to every pint, add 3 drachms of oil of spikenard; 1 drachm each of oil of thyme, lemon and clove, and a grain of civet and to 'shake well together before placing in a casting bottle'. This was a bottle made of porcelain and at the top were small holes to allow the water to be sprinkled over clothes. In wealthy homes, this was usually done by a servant when the guests arrived.

To make rose water, gather 1 lb (450 g) of petals of the most richly perfumed roses and after half filling a large kettle with water, drop in the petals and put on low heat. Fix a length of rubber tube about 4 ft (1 m) long to the spout of the kettle with the other end in a jar or bottle and with the middle portion of the tube submerged in ice cold water to cool the steam which will collect in the jar as pure rose water. Keep the kettle over the low heat until almost all the water has evaporated.

In several countries of the Near East, bottles of rose water (and the petals are often mixed with sweetly smelling herbs such as marjoram and basil) are placed on every table, to sprinkle over foods of every description whereas in Britain we have bottles of vinegar and Worcester sauce to use for the same purpose and in America, tomato sauce (catsup).

Sir Kenelm Digby, writing during the time of Charles II has given us an excellent recipe for a sweet water to use when washing the face and to sprinkle about an apartment. It is to take 2 handfuls each of Damask roses, basil, sweet rosemary and lavender and if possible, two walnut leaves (which have a pleasing resinous smell); a handful of rosemary tops and one of lemon balm, a few bay leaves, the peel of an orange or lemon and a few cloves. Place in a pan and fill up with 2 pt (1 litre) of white wine and leave for ten to twelve days. Then simmer for five minutes, strain and use a little of the liquid when required. It gives off a delicious scent.

To make a bath essence

An aromatic bath essence is made by boiling together the leaves of lavender, rosemary, bergamot and hyssop with chamomile flowers and the petals of red roses. Simmer for ten minutes over a low flame, strain into bottles and add a little alcohol in the form of whisky or brandy to give it a lasting perfume. Screw down the top and keep in a cupboard in the bathroom to use a little at a time in a warm bath. It will give the water a delicious 'herby' scent and will tone and relax the body. There are other herbs that can be used such as bay laurel, fennel, wild thyme, southernwood and pennyroyal but as with a *pot pourri*, it is a matter of preference and several different concoctions should be made up (taking note of the ingredients) to find out which is the most pleasing when used in the bath. A great deal of fun can be obtained by growing as many herbs as possible not only to use oneself but to make into sweet scented bags to give as presents, to place among clothes and under cushions and pillows for they will release a pleasing perfume when in contact with the warmth of the body.

In *The Toilet of Flora* is a recipe for a bath to cleanse and soften the skin. It is to boil together, 4 oz (110 g) of barley, 1 lb (450 g) of bran, two good sized handfuls of borage leaves and one of rosemary. Strain and add to a warm bath at bedtime. It will relax the body and the skin will be cleansed and made beautifully soft.

The same publication gives a reliable recipe for making an aromatic toilet vinegar. Put a handful of fresh rosemary or lavender or wormwood into an earthenware or glass jar and fill up with malt vinegar. Place in the sun for a week, then add 1 oz (28 g) of powdered camphor, strain off and bottle for use.

Another toilet vinegar is made by filling a large jar with red rose petals and sweet marjoram leaves, then top up with best vinegar. Leave in the sun for several days, strain off and bottle. If a little is added to a basinful of cold water and used for bathing the face and forehead during warm weather it will tighten the skin and remove wrinkles and be most refreshing. The *Toilet of Flora* gives a recipe to make lavender water. It is to simmer a handful of lavender flowers in a pint of water with the lid on the pan to retain the steam and until about half the water has evaporated. Then strain and use in washing water.

Sleep inducing herbs

In Ram's translation of Dodoen's *Herbal* is an interesting recipe for promoting sleep with dried rose leaves and mint. Dry and powder the mint, together with a teaspoonful of powdered cloves and mix with the rose petals. With the mixture, fill small muslin bags and place one under a pillowcase, when the warmth of the head will cause it to release a most pleasant perfume which induces deep sleep.

Sleep inducing herbs

A delightful sleep inducing pillow can be made by mixing together the dried leaves of bay laurel (only a few) with those of balm, southernwood, lemon thyme, bergamot and catmint, some chamomile flowers and hops. Some dried woodruff with its smell of coumarin should be added if it can be found. Add some dried and powdered lemon peel and a pinch of clove or cinnamon. Mix well together and fill a small pillow or a muslin bag which can be placed beneath a pillow case or inserted into a pillow containing flock or down. When warmed by the head it will release a gently soothing fragrance which will relieve nervous strain and bring about deep sleep.

Throughout their writings, the old herbalists mention the importance of pleasant smells to relieve a tired mind and to prevent depression. As William Coles said, 'Herbs comfort the wearied brain' and Gerard is for ever extolling the use of fragrant flowers and leaves about the home, in *pot pourris* and sweet scented waters. Of basil he wrote, 'The later writers ... do say that the smell of basil is good for the heart and to clear the head ... it taketh away sorrow that commeth with melancholie, and makes a man merrie and glad'. Of balm, John Evelyn wrote that it 'is sovereign for the brain, strengthening the memory and powerfully chasing away melancholy'. Of rosemary, Banche's *Herbal* (1525) says, 'the leaves laid under the pillow deliver one from evil dreams', presumably from melancholy thoughts and he advised one to 'smell it oft and it shall keep thee youngly'.

In *The Garden of Health* (1579), William Langham was equally enthusiastic about the many ways that rosemary could be used to 'gladden the heart' and prevent depression. He advised one 'to carry powder about thee, to make thee merry (refresh), glad, gracious, and well-beloved of all men ... seeth much rosemary and bottle the flowers, ... to make thee joyful, liking and youngly and to comfort the heart, boil the flowers in rose water, and drink it.'

Mary Eales, Confectioner to Queen Anne, in her *Book of Receipts* (1682) gives a delightful way of perfuming a room with rosemary. Take three teaspoonfuls of dried and powdered rosemary and as much sugar as would fill half a walnut (a teaspoonful). Scatter them in a warming pan placed over a low fire and soon the room will be filled with an aromatic perfume.

153

There were other ways of perfuming a room which could be followed today in those rooms where there is an open fire. Stevenson, in his *Calendar for Gardening* (1661) advised placing some angelica seeds into a warming pan (a clean frying pan will do) over a low fire or flame (perhaps a gas ring) when the pleasing scent would fill the whole house. A few leaves and twigs of bay laurel, thrown on to a low fire will produce the same effect and Dr Turner, Dean of Wells, who published the first part of his *Herbal* during the brief reign of Edward VI has told that the boy king's apartments were kept pleasantly scented by first burning juniper or cypress wood or elecampane roots over a low fire then later, fumigating with rose water and sugar in a warming pan, when the room smelled as though it was filled with roses.

Another pleasing way of scenting a room, and it is especially appreciated in a sick room, is to burn the stems of lavender flowers after the flowers have been removed. The 'sticks', which will be about 10 in (25 cm) long are first placed in a salt petre solution, then dried. They are stuck into bowls of sand and the other end is lit when the 'sticks' will burn slowly, like incense and give off a delicious lavender perfume. If the room is large, have two burning together, one at either end of the room. The 'sticks' will burn for several hours if draughts are excluded from the room.

Pots of lavender and rosemary were to be found in the mullioned windows of most homes for they were able to absorb heat in summer and so kept the rooms cool, while suppressing the often unpleasant smell of dampness. Isaac Walton paints a delightful picture of 'the honest alehouse, where we shall find a clean room with lavender in the windows'. But long before, Sir Hugh Platt had written that to keep rooms cool and pleasant smelling, pots of rosemary should be kept in a fireplace in summertime when they would hide an empty grate and absorb the summer heat of a room with a low ceiling. Bunches of herbs were hung from the ceiling of rooms for much the same purpose. In earlier times and until the middle of the nineteenth century, herbs were in constant use for this purpose and for providing the home with their pleasing perfumes in exactly the same way that they were used to cure simple ailments, to tone up the system and to add their individual flavours to culinary practice.

Herbs to use in moist and dry *pot pourris*

Herb	Botanical name	Use
Bergamot	*Monarda didyma*	Pot pourris; sweet bags
Balm	*Melissa officinalis*	Moist and dry *pot pourris*
Costmary	*Chrysanthemum balsamita*	Pot pourris; sweet bags
Fragrant Agrimony	*Agrimonia odorata*	Pot pourris; scented pillows
Lavender	*Lavendula spica*	Pot pourris; sweet bags; washing waters
Orange Thyme	*Thymus fragrantissimus*	Pot pourris; sweet bags
Orris root	*Iris florentina*	Sweet powders
Red rose	*Rosa gallica officinalis*	Pot pourris; sweet bags; rose water
Rosemary	*Rosmarinus officinalis*	Sweet bags; *pot pourris;* scented waters
Rose Root	*Sedum rosea*	For rose water
Southernwood	*Artemisia abrotanum*	Pot pourris; sweet bags
Sweet Basil	*Ocimum basilicum*	Pot pourris; sweet bags
Sweet Marjoram	*Origanum majorana*	Sweet powders; *pot pourris*; sweet waters
Woodruff	*Asperula odorata*	Pot pourris; scented pillows; sweet waters

Herbs that when dried are moth deterrent

Cotton lavender	Southernwood
Featherfew	Tansy
Mugwort	Thyme
Rosemary	Woodruff
Rue	Wormwood

Herbs (fresh) to keep flies away

Anise	Peppermint
Basil	Rue
Chamomile	Tansy
Mugwort	Yarrow
Pennyroyal	Yellow Loosestrife

Herbs (fresh) to freshen the air of a room

Balm	Lavender
Bay	Mint(s)
Germander	Rosemary
Hyssop	Thyme

Herbs (fresh) for a fragrant bath

Agrimony	Lavender
Bay	Sweet Marjoram
Bergamot	Mugwort
Chamomile	Pennyroyal
Germander	Rosemary
Ground Ivy	Water Mint

Herbs to make sweet-scented bags

Agrimony	Red Rose
Hyssop	Rosemary
Lavender	Sweet Marjoram

Glossary of Terms

Annual	A plant which matures in the same year its seed is sown, as caraway, dill.
Anti-scorbutic	Plants capable of supplying the body with Vitamin C which keeps it free from scurvy.
Astringent	Tightening. Applied internally to the staying of loose bowels and externally, to tighten the skin (face).
Axil	The upper angle formed by leaf and stem.
Axillary	Borne in the axils of the leaves.
Biennial	A plant which matures the year after the seed is sown, as with borage, clary.
Bracts	Small (modified) leaves present on flower stalks.
Calyx	The green whorl of leaf-like organs of a flower.
Capitate	Heads, as in Compositae.
Capsule	A dry, many-seeded vessel.
Cordate	Heart-shaped leaf with rounded lobes at the base.
Corymb	Raceme of flowers on pedicels which decrease in length as they reach the top of the stem.
Cutting	A woody shoot removed from a plant for rooting.
Cyme	Terminal inflorescence beneath which are side branches bearing a terminal flower.
Deciduous	A tree, shrub or plant losing its leaves each year.

Decurrent	Where the leaf blade is continued downwards on petiole or stem.
Demulcent	Soothing and healing to the stomach.
Dentate	Leaves with triangular teeth at the margins.
Disc	Central florets of Compositae, as in daisy.
Diuretic	To cleanse the kidneys of impurities.
Down	White hairs which cover leaves and sometimes the stems as with mullein.
Elliptic	Oblong leaves with blunt ends.
Entire	Leaves neither divided nor toothed at the margins.
Evergreen	Tree, shrub or plant retaining its leaves through winter.
Florets	Outer or rayed petals of a flower as in Compositae (e.g. daisy, featherfew).
Glabrous	Smooth, glossy, without hairs, used to describe certain plants (e.g. soapwort).
Glandular	A cell secreting essential oil.
Glaucous	Leaves which have a blueish appearance (e.g. rue).
Heel	A thin piece of bark or wood attached to a cutting.
Involucre	Whorled bracts at the base of a flower.
Labiate	Lipped; when the corolla of a flower is divided into two unequal parts, as in mint, lavender, marjoram, sage.
Lanceolate	Lance-shaped leaves, tapering at the end.
Node	A point on the stem where a leaf is produced and from which the stem may root when in contact with the soil as with ground ivy.
Opposite	A term describing leaves which appear opposite each other on a stem.
Pappus	A hairy appendage of a seed.
Pedicil	Stalk of a flower of floret.
Pellucid	Transparent dots or glands of a leaf containing the essential oil.
Perennial	A plant of more than two years duration but

usually a term used for those plants of far longer duration as with balm, cowslip.

Petiole	The stalk of a leaf where it joins the main stem.
Pratense	Growing in meadows.
Pubescent	Leaves and stems covered in hairs or down.
Raceme	Stalked flowers, borne in a spike.
Radical	Leaves arising from just above the roots rather than on a stem.
Rosette	Leaves radiating from a central underground stem as with Lady's Smock.
Segment	Part of a leaf divided almost to the mid-rib.
Serrate	Saw- or toothed-edged leaves.
Simple	Leaves not divided.
Solitary	Flowers borne singly, one to a stalk.
Spike	As raceme, except that the flowers are stalkless.
Stamen	Male organ of a flower – filament and anther.
Stigma	Cellular part at top of a style to which pollen adheres.
Style	Termination of a carpel bearing the stigma.
Tomentose	Covered with silky hairs.
Umbel	Stalked flowers arising from one point and reaching to about the same level.
Whorl	Flowers or leaves arranged in a circle around a stem.

Further Reading List

Amherst, Hon. Alicia, *A History of Gardening in England* (Bernard Quaritch, 1895)

Brownlow, Margaret, *Herbs and the Fragrant Garden* (Darton Longman & Todd, 1957)

Culpeper, Nicholas, *The English Physician* (William Cole, 1652)

Fernie, Dr W. T., *Herbal Simples* (John Wright, 1894)

Fernie, Dr W. T., (Third and revised Edition of *Herbal Simples*) (John Wright, 1914)

Genders, Roy, *The History of Scent* (Hamish Hamilton, 1972)

Genders, Roy, *The Scented Wild Flowers of Britain* (Collins, 1971)

Grieve, Mrs and Leyel, Mrs, *A Modern Herbal* (Jonathan Cape, 1931; 1977)

Hampton, F. A., *The Scent of Flowers and Leaves* (Dulau & Co, 1925)

Hewer, D. G., *Practical Herb Growing* (G. Bell, 1941)

Holmes, E. M., *Profitable Herb Growing and Collecting* (Geo Newnes, 1916)

McDonald, Donald, *Sweet Scented Flowers* (Sampson Low, 1895)

Moldenke, Harold and Alma, *Plants of the Bible* (Ronald Press, New York, 1952)

Northcote, Lady Rosalind, *The Book of Herbs* (The Bodley Head, 1902)

Pechey, John, (1694), *English Herbal of Physical Plants* (reprint) (Medical Publications, 1951)

Quelch, Mary Thorne, *Herbs and How to Know Them* (Faber & Faber, 1946)

Rohde, Eleanor Sinclair, *Culinary and Salad Herbs* (Country Life, 1940)

Rohde, Eleanor Sinclair, *Herbs and Herb Gardening* (Medici Society, 1936)

Rohde, Eleanor Sinclair, *The Old English Herbals* (reprint) (Minerva Press, 1972)

Rohde, Eleanor Sinclair, *The Scented Garden* (Medici Society, 1931)

Shewell-Cooper, W. E., *Plants and Fruits of the Bible* (Darton Longman & Todd, 1957)

Tudor, Alice, *A Little Book of Healing Herbs* (Medici Society, 1927)

Whitehead, George E., *Garden Herbs* (A. & C. Black, 1942)

Metric/Imperial Equivalents

Temperature

°F	°C
45	7
50	10
55	13
60	16
65	18
70	21

Length

in	cm
$\frac{1}{4}$	0·5
$\frac{1}{2}$	1·0
1	2·5
12	30
24	60

Weight

oz/sq yd	g/m²	oz	g
1	35	1	28
2	70	4	113
3	100	16 (1 lb)	454
4	140	36 ($2\frac{1}{4}$ lb)	1000 (1 Kg)

Area

1 sq yd = 0·8 m²
$1\frac{1}{4}$ sq yd = 1·0 m²

Volume

pints	litres
$\frac{1}{2}$	0·3
1	0·6
$1\frac{3}{4}$	1·0

Note: These conversions are approximate.

Index

Index

Index

Index

Sprains, herbs to ease 45, 64, 132
St John's Wort 6, 67, 71, 122, 144
   culture 67
Stachys betonica, see Wood Betony
Stomach pains, to ease 82
Strewing, herbs for 7, 15, 41, 51, 63, 80
Stuffing, herbs for 7, 9, 38, 43, 45, 48, 57, 61, 68, 81, 99, 102
Succory, *see* Chicory
Sweet bags 8, 11, 23, 36, 38, 42, 45, 63, 146, 148, 155, 156
Sweet Cicely 15, 85, 100, 103
   culture 100
Sweet Fern 100
Sweet water 11, 44, 151

Tansy 6, 7, 11, 15, 67, 71, 155
   culture 68
   in drinks 7
Tansy cakes 7, 67
Taraxacum officinalis, see Dandelion
Tarragon, French 68, 71
   freezing 68
   propagation 68
   vinegar 68, 96, 126
Teas, herbal 2, 7, 23, 43, 51, 55, 56, 57, 58, 59, 66, 68, 76, 78, 81, 82, 91, 95, 120, 132, 140
Teucrium chamaedrys, see Germander
Thyme
   common 27, 50, 52, 155
   culture 50
   golden 18, 27, 51
   oil of 15, 82
   prostrate 76
Thymol 82
Thymus azaricus 80
Thymus doerfleri 79
Thymus drucei, see Wild Thyme
Thymus fragrantissimus 80, 148
Thymus herba-barona 80, 82
Thymus nitidus 80
Thymus serpyllus, see Mountain thyme
Toilet vinegar 151
Tonic beers 87, 120, 132, 134
Tonic drinks 8, 44, 48, 55, 56, 61, 68, 69, 87, 132, 133, 141

Tragopogon porrifolius, see Salsify
Tree onion 85, 103
Tropaeolum majus, see Nasturtium
Turner, William 12, 58, 96, 154
Tusser, Thomas 7, 12, 40, 51, 80, 91, 128
Tussilago farfara, see Coltsfoot

Urtica dioica, see Nettle

Valerian 141, 143
   culture 143
Valerianella locusta, see Lamb's Lettuce
Vegetables, herbs as 2, 9, 26, 104, 121, 128
Verbascum thapsus, see Mullein
Verbena officinalis, see Vervain
Vervain 69, 71
   culture 69
Vinca minor, see Lesser Periwinkle
Vitamins 2, 16, 63, 96, 98

Walton, Isaac 43, 154
Watercress 100, 103
   culture 101
Waters, scented 11
White Briony 139, 143
Wild thyme 81, 82, 83
Window box 27
   herbs for 29
   its construction 28
Winter Radish 113, 114
   culture 113
Witchcraft, herbs in 6, 69
Wood Avens, *see* Herb Bennet
Wood Betony 69, 140, 143
   culture 140
Woodruff 8, 133, 140, 143, 149, 155
Wormwood, Common 3, 6, 8, 17, 24, 35, 52, 146, 155
Wormwood, Roman 18, 46, 52

Yellow gentian 19, 69, 71
   propagation 69
Yellow loosestrife 3, 21, 70
   propagation 70, 71